CW01511286

# Praise
## *What You Seek is*

"*What You Seek Is Seeking You is a transformational experience that will change your life forever. We have entered a time in our evolution where we are being called to live up to a higher set of values—authenticity, gratitude, courage, compassion, mindfulness, and generosity. This beautiful book is a powerful expression of that call, with a liberating and empowering message delivered in an easily digestible format.*"

— JACK CANFIELD, # 1 bestselling author of *The Success Principles* and co-author of *Chicken Soup for the Soul series*

"*You'll love the creative way Jamal and Tracy teach in this book the principles and fundamentals for a life filled with success and framed with significance. Both have coached millions —and now it's your turn to tap into their wisdom.*"

— DR. NIDO R. QUBEIN, President, High Point University, North Carolina, USA

"*A fascinating book filled with valuable lessons and powerful insights that will fuel your success.*"

— ROBIN SHARMA, #1 bestselling author of *The Leader Who Had No Title* and founder of The Titan Academy

"*Leave it to Brian Tracy and Azim Jamal, two master practitioners and teachers, to provide us with such profound wisdom in the form of a combination parable and how-to learning guide. Not only will this book reach into your heart and soul and touch it deeply; it will also provide you with the instructions on how to dramatically increase your joy, peace of mind, confidence and earning potential. Magnificent!*"

— BOB BURG, co-author of the national bestseller, *The Go-Giver*

"I've long admired both Brian Tracy and Azim Jamal. It's wonderful that they have combined their deep experience and wisdom to help you discover what you most desire and deserve in life."

— HARVEY MCKINNON, author of *Hidden Gold* and # 1 bestselling co-author of *The Power of Giving*

"A must-read by Jamal and Tracy who captivate messages promoting uber success–in business and life–all grounded in values desired by all who dream about a well rounded successful life!"

— MALIK TALIB, CEO, All Asia Fresh Foods, Inc. and Board Member, Vancouver Foundation

"Practical, Inspiring, Insightful, Enriching! A must-read for leaders at all levels!"

— NICK NANTON, Three-time Emmy Award Winning Director and Wall Street Journal Bestselling Author

"A timeless piece of work and a recipe for a beautiful life by Jamal & Tracy. This book provokes reflection and will spark a positive change in your thoughts, feelings, actions & results. The lessons are simple yet powerful!"

— MUBEEN KHAN, CEO, African Billionaire Events Management

"At last, a book that finally helps us understand that the success we seek is actually seeking us. This book is practical, innovative, creative and full of wisdom. Buy and read this book and you will learn to harness one of the great secrets of life. Learn from Brian Tracy and Azim Jamal. I do!"

— DR. PETER LEGGE, OBC, CPAE, LLD (HON.), Chairman & CEO, Canada Wide Media Limited

# WHAT
# YOU SEEK
## IS
# SEEKING
# YOU

# WHAT
# YOU SEEK
## IS
# SEEKING
# YOU

## BRIAN TRACY
## AZIM JAMAL

# JAICO PUBLISHING HOUSE

Ahmedabad Bangalore Chennai
Delhi Hyderabad Kolkata Mumbai

Published by Jaico Publishing House
A-2 Jash Chambers, 7-A Sir Phirozshah Mehta Road
Fort, Mumbai - 400 001
jaicopub@jaicobooks.com
www.jaicobooks.com

Published in arrangement with
Brian Tracy
320 Loma Larga Drive
Solana Beach, CA, 92075, USA
&
Azim Jamal
Founder & CEO
Corporate Sufi Worldwide
10151 Gilmore Crescent
Richmond, BC V6X 1X1, Canada

To be sold only in India, Bangladesh, Bhutan,
Pakistan, Nepal, Sri Lanka and the Maldives.

WHAT YOU SEEK IS SEEKING YOU
ISBN 978-81-8495-744-0

First Jaico Impression: 2015
Third Jaico Impression: 2017

Page design and layout: Ramdas Lal, Delhi

Printed by
Trinity Academy For Corporate Training Limited, Mumbai

# Contents

# Preface

*"If it is bread that you seek, you will have bread,*
*If it is the soul you seek, you will find the soul.*
*If you understand this secret, you know you are that which you*
*seek."*

– Rumi (12<sup>th</sup> century Sufi poet)

You are a part of existence, and all your dreams and desires are already part of your existential consciousness. The universe endorses your dreams. Rumi, in the quote above, is telling us to hold on to our dreams, because dreams are the road map to growth and evolution.

After working with senior executives and coaching business leaders for decades, we have discovered that leaders at all levels continuously seek improvement in their business; strive for the elusive work-life balance; and search for purpose and happiness. The most successful leaders face challenges throughout their journey and struggle to find a deeper meaning of life.

However, what you seek has always been seeking you, even if you haven't realized it. This is how the universe is designed. If you've spent your entire life blind to this fact, you don't have to continue staying in the dark anymore. You can sharpen your awareness, commit to your goals and understand that what you truly need is already available to you.

In his younger days, Brian went through difficult times, struggling with different jobs and even living out of his car, before finding the secret of success. His life took an unexpected turn, and he became a top personal development, business and sales guru, helping many individuals and corporations – including his own companies – create multimillion-dollar businesses in the process. Azim was a successful accountant with three professional degrees, but something was missing. He then found the perfect recipe to live a purposeful, successful and well-balanced life in the eastern philosophy of Sufism. He switched from accounting for business to accounting for life, and went on to share his unique Corporate Sufi message with millions around the world. Both writers discovered that what they were seeking was also seeking them.

In this book, they share insightful and tangible ways to:

- enhance your business acumen
- convert corporate politics into creative synergy
- be authentic in everything you do
- embrace meditation and inner peace
- invite positive coincidences and attract what you seek

- set goals, remain focused and yet stay detached from the outcome

- be fully committed to your vision and long-term plans, yet be in the present moment

- transform ego (which is a negative force) into positive pride. Brian and Azim portray business and life concepts using a fable as the backdrop. To help readers through the process, they have also shared messages after each chapter, and have included 'Reflection' and 'How to' exercises to reinforce the changes to be made. For example, it is one thing to have read, heard and spoken about being in the present moment, but completely another to actually be there, especially when you are stressed out or meeting a deadline. Life, like business, is always a work in progress, never a finished product. No matter how successful you are, you can still get better.

To access these benefits, you must be open-minded, implement what you learn and realize that what *you* are seeking is also seeking *you*!

**Enjoy!**

**Brian Tracy & Azim Jamal**

# Chapter One

# Experiencing the Freedom
# of Authenticity

*"Each friend represents a world in us, a world not born until they arrive, and it is only by this meeting that a new world is born."*

– Anais Nin

The VIP lounge at Delhi Airport was milling with people and strange smells. The morning flight to Turkey had been delayed due to fog, and airlines were scrambling to placate impatient passengers with complimentary breakfast coupons. There was already a steady stream of people making their way into the café next to the lounge. Richard held his plate of food protectively with one hand and balanced his travel bag with the other. He looked around for an empty chair, and found one near a table at the further end of the cafe.

There was an Asian woman sitting alone at the table near a large bay window, watching the view outside. Normally, Richard would have resisted the idea of sharing a table with a stranger; the need to introduce oneself, followed by the customary round of polite conversation, were social obligations he would gladly avoid. But he was famished, and if a perfunctory chat could secure him a seat, he was okay with it.

"Excuse me, are you expecting someone? If not, may I join you?" Richard asked politely.

Zoya seemed a little startled, but quickly recovered and looked up at the stranger, inviting him to take a seat with a smile. She noticed he was dressed in a charcoal grey suit and dark blue silk tie and he had steady blue eyes.

Richard sat down before the lady could change his mind. He balanced his bag against the leg of the table and began tearing his plastic cutlery wrap.

"I couldn't find a place to sit," he explained hurriedly, "and I really have some important work to do."

"I'm not expecting anyone," she replied calmly. "Thanks

for asking though," she added after a little pause, with a hint of a smile. It was then that Richard noticed her eyes. Large and dark, they were twinkling with amusement.

He started to eat, carefully slicing the rice cake with surgical precision, his mind deep in thought over his forthcoming presentation.

"If only the board would agree to invest, the company would be able to continue the development. The new metal alloy that the design team was working on had showed good potential. If only..." he thought, shoving a forkful of rice cake in his mouth.

"You should try that with *sambhar*. It'll taste better."

"Excuse me?" Richard asked, a little taken aback.

"You should try the *idlis* with some *sambhar*. That's the yellow curry by the side of your potatoes. *Idlis* taste better when eaten with the curry."

"Oh, thank you, but I am afraid Indian spices don't agree with my digestion," he replied with a trace of polite indifference, hoping she wouldn't bother him anymore.

"Oh ok. Well, then try it with some butter. My niece loves it that way," Zoya persisted, passing her tiny tray of butter to Richard.

He looked up and started to say something curt to put an end to her pleasantries, but then she smiled again. She seemed to be in her early thirties, with a slender frame and long dark hair. She wore a deep blue Indian kurta with fitted jeans, and silver bangles on her arm. She was dribbling generous spoonfuls of honey on her toast and caught Richard looking at her.

"Would you like to have some?" she asked, beginning to offer him the honey.

"Er, no!" he said quickly, pulling back his food tray a little.

"So traveling to Turkey for work? Or is it a vacation?" she inquired.

"Work," he answered, and went back to slicing his *idlis* intently. But she didn't take the hint.

"Business meeting?"

He sighed and put down his fork.

"Kind of. Attending a sales conference," he answered.

"Interesting!" she nodded. "If I might ask, what business are you in?"

"We design and manufacture metal automotive components and chassis for vehicle bodies. Chassis is the internal framework of a car... like a skeleton," he explained, hoping a detailed explanation about how automobiles are manufactured would put her off further questions.

"So are you in charge of marketing?" she asked, undeterred.

"No, I am the CEO," he answered forcefully, and then wondered if that came across as too arrogant. But may be that would put an end to her chatter.

"Cool!" she exclaimed. "So how's the industry doing right now? Is the auto market going through a slump?" she inquired, heaping butter on another piece of toast.

"It is. But then every business goes through its cycles."

"This too shall pass," he added, lifting his shoulders nonchalantly.

"It will, it always does," she answered smiling, and then leaned forward and added, "Yet isn't it strange, how worked up we all get whenever there is even a little slide in the stock market?"

"Well, I think it's easy for someone who is not wondering where his or her next paycheck is coming from," he stated a little pointedly.

"I agree. But I guess we derive special joy in ratcheting up bad news. I mean, look at this news channel," she said, pointing to the flat screen on the wall next to their table.

"They have been discussing the economic slowdown since the past one hour, and every 10 minutes, they invite yet another expert, from yet another sector, to comment on the economy. And Mr. Expert then goes over his dreary monologue, drawing gloomy little squiggles on falling graphs and doling out an even gloomier outlook."

Richard forced back a smile.

"You might have a point. But even the analyst there has to make a living," he said.

"But not at the expense of making all of us morose," she said, lifting her eyebrows.

"It's like this morbid fascination we have with the idea of doomsday. I mean look at our movies. I think more than 50 percent of popular films today are about the end of the world, either brought about by Godzillas, giant machines, or monstrous aliens. Sometimes I think, we are all unwittingly involved in this conspiracy to create a constant state of fear.

"And since no aliens seem to be attacking us, we start creating monsters in our own backyards. One day it's the innocuous-looking wheat wreaking havoc on our bodies with gluten, or apples filling us up with insecticides. The next day, it's the sun giving us skin cancer or lack of vitamin D giving rise to all sorts of ailments. Basically, the central idea is to run scared as the universe is out to get you!"

"A lot of it is true."

"Yes, it is. But then, not all that is said on television is the truth. Unless you are planning to binge on bread, I don't think the poor bread is out to get you," she explained, raising her hands.

"Well, you always have the choice to ignore these ideas," he countered.

"Yes we do, but not when they are being shoved down our throats 24/7. Look at our newspapers – there are endless stories about things going wrong in the world. But life is not really like that, is it? I mean we don't have just bad days. In fact, even in a day, we have so many moments that make us smile."

Richard sighed. She seemed like one of those post-modern hippies out to transform the world, one fellow passenger at a time. And today was his turn. Ordinarily, he would have shut her up with a pointed remark, but the fact that he was sharing her table dampened his eagerness for a rebuttal. Agreement seemed to be the only smart defense.

"Hmm, you are right," he said, nodding his head at her thoughtfully and then peering at his plate, hoping his response was enough to quell her sense of injustice with the world.

But she seemed to be a lady with a mission, living her *Joan of Arc* moment.

"You know, a newspaper vendor in my area is supporting

the education of three children in his slum. Children who are not even related to him. Why can't we print such news? The good bits, the parts which make you want to believe in life again. But it seems we, as a society, seem to be obsessed with bad news. I feel–," she began.

"So why do you think we have this morbid fascination with fear?" he interrupted, leaning back his six-foot-one frame over the chair, and suddenly pulling back a little after bumping his legs into Zoya's under the table.

"Because it feeds our ego," replied Zoya, dunking a slice of lime in her watermelon juice.

"We scare ourselves to death because it feeds our ego? I thought ego was supposed to make us feel superior, arrogant?" Richard asked with a trace of irritation mingled with curiosity.

"Well, ego is not simply a superiority complex. It's your sense of separateness from the rest of the world. Anything that strengthens this separation, this feeling of difference, feeds the ego. And fear always makes you distant from everybody else," she answered. "I mean, we are all essentially alone in our fears."

"Hmm… but fear alerts us to the possibility of danger," he replied.

"Yes, but most of the time we carry a lot of anxiety to simply indulge ourselves. Fear is like a security blanket we drag along, hoping it will somehow protect us from the uncertainty of life."

"Fear as security blankets?" he asked, ladling some butter on to his *idli*.

"Well, don't you think our fears prevent us from living, expanding our experience? We can hide behind them and avoid exploring anything new or strange," replied Zoya.

"Hmm," he said, chewing thoughtfully and enjoying the balmy flavor of the butter gently flooding his mouth.

"Plus, fear makes great fodder for armchair conversations," she added.

He raised an eyebrow.

"I mean, it feels great to sip your green tea and postulate endless theories about the sorry state of the world," she said rolling her eyes and added, "be it politics, or the economy or even weight gain. Then once we have intellectualized everything, we can end the discussion with the classic eulogy to the good old times; as if we are somehow closer to decoding life. And the funny part is we never get around to doing much about what bothers us anyway. Next day, it's the same old story and the same old regrets."

"Or it's about how the world is not ready for us; how people don't understand us; or how obtuse the world is becoming," Richard said.

"Exactly!" she beamed.

"Hmm, funny that we don't realize the irony. Probably, it would be a good idea to take a step back and think about our conversations and find out if we really are all that different. Some green tea for you?" he asked, and lifted his hand to signal the waiter.

She stared at him for a long moment and then burst out laughing.

"Wow, you are good!

He said with a smile, "I don't know what you are talking about."

"You are right! I have been complaining like everybody else. Complaining about things is just another way of adding to the morbidity. It doesn't really change anything," said Zoya.

The waiter, who had been hovering for some time now, immediately approached their table. Richard asked for a coffee refill and Zoya asked for another bottle of water.

"So what's your version of the perfect world?" he asked, curious to see what new utopian ideal she wanted to peddle.

"Nothing. I think it already is."

"Really? Now that's a first," he said, raising one eyebrow and leaning his head forward on his hand.

"All I want is the freedom to be happy about life. Freedom to explore, to feel good about myself as I am, and not when I weigh a certain number of pounds, or look a certain way, or reach a particular post in my job."

"So what's stopping you?"

"Nothing I guess," she added slowly. "But sometimes I feel swamped, when the whole world is bent on proving how you need to be more successful, more aggressive and wealthier to be happy.

"It's always how you need to be *more*… and if you are not, you'd better not be happy. Somehow, it's more normal to be miserable than to be happy, don't you think?" asked Zoya.

She sighed, looking a little lost, even forlorn, for a moment. But she recovered and looked back at him eagerly. He wondered what she will say now.

"Anyway, coming back to your business, are you also looking at drawing sorry little squiggles in your conference?"

"On the contrary, we are projecting a rise in sales," he said, smiling calmly.

"Interesting! How is that?"

"We are working on a new metal alloy which is expected to lighten the chassis weight by at least…"

*Why am I telling her all this?* Richard wondered, leaning sideways to remove his reading glasses and passport from his trouser pocket, and shoving them in his inner coat pocket.

"At least?" she asked, leaning forward.

"Well, we are still working on it," he answered a little tersely.

She looked at him for what seemed like a long moment and started to smile, but then held back and lowered her gaze, as if sensing his sudden discomfort. There was silence. Neither spoke for some time.

"So what do *you* do?" he asked, finally giving in.

"Me? I am an artist. I paint. And occasionally, I freelance as an illustrator for children's books," she answered.

"Interesting. So did you always want to be a painter?"

"I think I was always a painter. Even when I didn't know it. But my family was all set for me to become an engineer. They felt it was more stable, more respectable. Even my friends were a little shocked when I chose to study art instead of engineering. And to be honest, initially, even I was a little unsure. Maybe they were right. Maybe I would end up hungry and homeless, painting outdoor signs for a living. But I eventually decided to follow my heart." She gestured towards the table. "Your sleeve."

"Huh?" he said, looking around, feeling a little fazed. She should stop smiling, he thought, it's distracting.

"Your sleeve is dipping into the chutney."

"Oh, damn!" he exclaimed, pulling back his sleeve, aware of the yellow stain fast spreading on the cuff of his starched white shirt.

At 38, Richard cut an attractive figure and had the unassuming confidence that comes with knowing that he looked presentable. He had a Nordic bearing with clear blue eyes and blonde hair, which he liked to keep short. Moreover, his regular features and square jaw presented a solid image – one that kept the press photographers happy and his shareholders calm. Hence, he never felt the need to waste too much time on deliberating what to wear or eat. Both for him were just means to an end.

But he was fastidious about cleanliness. Everything had to be neat, precise and in its place. The thought of carrying on the rest of the day with a stained cuff annoyed him.

"By the way, I am Zoya Rahman," she said, extending her hand.

"Richard. Richard Wiseman," he answered.

## Bringing It to Life: Messages from Chapter One – Experiencing the Freedom of Authenticity

### *The Storyline*

Zoya has chosen to be a painter and follow her heart. Choosing to do what she loves makes her feel authentic.

### *Messages*

As Steve Jobs said: "Your time is limited, so don't waste it living someone else's life. Don't be trapped by dogma – which is living with the results of other people's thinking. Don't let the noise of others' opinions drown your own inner voice. And most importantly, have the courage to follow your heart and intuition. They somehow already know what you truly want to become. Everything else is secondary."

### *Reflect on the following questions:*

- Do you really believe everything you say to your family, team, customers, and stakeholders?

- Do you go deep enough to explore your motives in what you do at work, home, in the community, with your friends?

- Have you discovered your innate gift and passion?

- Are you clear as to what is unique about you and your business (your personal and corporate brand)?

- Do you accept yourself unconditionally, imperfections and all?

- Do you walk your talk?

- Are you transparent?

- Do you genuinely care about your team and customers?

- Do you admit to mistakes and apologize as required, (building trust vs. defensiveness)?

- Before embarking on something, do you ask yourself: Does this feel right to me?

Your inner light shines through you when you are credible and trustworthy, and honest enough to admit to your limitations. The reality is that even with all your limitations, you are still unique and special. Embrace who you are, flaws and all. If you try to be someone else, you only become a 'second-best someone'. As they say: "Be yourself. Everyone else is already taken."

The power of authentic leadership was captured in a study published in 2007 in *The Harvard Business Review*. The study – which polled over 100 business leaders aged 23 to 95, chosen for their reputations among their peer groups for authenticity in leadership – found that there was no single personal trait that made the leaders appear authentic to their peers. Rather, there was a technique common among these leaders – they "were constantly testing themselves through real-world experiences and reframing their life stories to understand who they were at their core. In doing so, they discovered the purpose of their leadership and learned how being authentic made them more effective."

A lot of people fear being themselves because they feel they won't be liked or accepted. If someone likes you when you are living a lie, he may stop associating with you when he finds out the real you; because sooner or later, truth reveals itself. By pretending to be someone you are not just for garnering attention, you are most likely to end up attracting the wrong people.

Not being yourself can also lead to a no-win situation. If you are not a genuine expression of yourself, the acclaim of your colleagues and your friends will amount to little. It is important that you like yourself first, and that can only happen if you allow yourself to be true to your inner being. As Shakespeare aptly said: "…to thine own self be true, and it must follow, as the night the day, thou canst not then be false to any man…"

Admitting your mistakes won't torpedo your career; in fact, those who are able to admit mistakes, often bounce back from these career upsets quicker than those who try to cover up. Take the case of John F Kennedy, whose frank public admission of failure in the wake of the 1961 Bay of Pigs fiasco helped him to maintain his popularity with voters and go down in history as one of America's most beloved presidents.

Costco co-founder and former CEO, Jim Sinegal, led his company to impressive returns until his retirement in 2011. Though Sinegal was one of the most successful CEOs in

America, his modesty at the company headquarters – he answered his own phone line, maintained a small office, paid himself a salary far lower than that of his peers in the industry and wore a nametag that simply said, 'Jim' – made him wildly popular with his employees, and left him with an employee turnover rate that was among the lowest in the entire retail industry.

Many of the most remarkable and successful people show that the benefits of being true to oneself and one's beliefs far outpace those of simply aping everyone else's values:

Warren Buffett invested more than 90 percent of his personal savings as a show of confidence when he was recruiting backers for one of his first investment partnerships, in the early 60s. Buffet's trust in himself, and willingness to put his own money and career on the line, are part of what has led to the success of his career.

– During the recession of the 1970s, Hewlett-Packard co-founder Bill Hewlett took a 10 percent pay cut, the same as all of his employees. This created a positive environment for workers at Hewlett-Packard, which exists to this day – an expectation that management is working with them, not against them, and wants everyone to succeed.

– Wal-Mart founder Sam Walton rented the same economy cars and stayed in the same economy hotels as his employees when he traveled for work. This gesture, which showed that Walton viewed himself as part of the team, rather than above his employees, contributed to the company's growth and success.

– McDonald's founder Ray Kroc expected all employees to help keep McDonald's clean and didn't exempt himself from the job – he picked up garbage found in parking lots of every McDonald's outlet that he visited.

If you want your success to be sustainable, if you want it to have a strong foundation, if you want it to have purpose and meaning, there is no other way than to be authentic.

Authenticity isn't just the key to a long-lasting career; it's the key to developing real, meaningful power. In addition, charisma is one of the most important factors that help establish a business career but when it's not tethered to a solid sense of your credibility, it can lead to hazardous and even evil behavior. Hitler and Stalin possessed charisma but because their values were heinous, that charisma only led to evil.

Jordan Belfort (the corrupt stockbroker whose crimes were dramatized in the film, *The Wolf of Wall Street*) and Bernard Madoff were shrewd, articulate and charismatic, but they used their charisma to swindle people out of their life savings. Both these men had power but it was not tethered to good, authentic values. Real power can only truly come from authenticity. As Dr. Nido Qubein, President of North Carolina University and a good friend of ours, would say: "Charisma is good, but charisma without authenticity is dangerous."

*Challenge yourself with the following 'How to' exercises:*

1. ACCEPT and realize your imperfections – shortcomings are part of who you are. Realizing this

makes you powerful because you can understand others, relate to them and help them based on what you've learned and realized from your own shortcomings. At work, this kind of acceptance will help you learn from every mistake you make, and become more open to feedback, guidance and constructive criticism. This acceptance will shift your goals from "how can I protect my flaws from being discovered" to "how can I get better."

2.  APPRECIATE yourself more as a person (both the positive and negative qualities) to gain confidence in expressing yourself. Remember your successes – at school, at home, in sports, art and in the community. Remember that some of the greats like Einstein, in their youth, were believed to have no potential!

3.  LIVE a life of honesty and integrity. How can you tell if you're succeeding in this? Ask yourself that exact question. Your initial reaction will often be that you are, but go deeper. Because it's likely that you will be succeeding in some areas, but not in others. Don't be discouraged by this, however. View it as an opportunity to grow.

4.  KNOW THAT BEING DIFFERENT is good. Your unique selling proposition (USP) comes from being different and unique. Achievers like Michael Jordan, Steve Jobs and JK Rowling were often regarded as either eccentric, reckless or suffering from an attention disorder.

5.  RADIATE CONFIDENCE – When you are authentic, you can have confidence that the people in your life

who are not aligned with you are not supposed to be in your life anyway.

6. BE NON-JUDGEMENTAL – Be careful about judging others because you do not know what they are going through. Every time a celebrity is revealed to have been severely suffering we are caught off guard. For example, actor Robin Williams' suicide shocked most of us because he seemed to have everything a person could wish for – fame, money and talent. But just because we see someone's external successes does not mean that we have seen their inner life.

7. ADMIT mistakes and apologize because this builds trust. This is hard for most of us to practice because we fear that we may appear incompetent. However, small inadequacies in life are normal and can be accepted by almost everyone. Dishonesty and cover-ups are far worse.

8. PRACTICE COURAGE – Speak the truth, allow yourself to be vulnerable and step out of your comfort zone. For example, in a staff meeting, ask for help if you need it, ask a question (that you may be afraid to ask), speak up about a concern or issue you may have. Don't worry about what others may think.

If you have a question that you need to ask in order to be clear about something, chances are someone else too has the same question. By asking, you make others in your team admire your courage. It also reveals to your leader that you are not afraid to ask questions, and that you're willing to risk embarrassment in order to seek clarification, instead of pretending to have understood and later going off the rails.

9.  BE TRUE TO YOURSELF – Before embarking on something, ask: Does this feel right to me? When you are true to yourself, you are generally true to others.

# Chapter Two

# Attracting Positive Coincidences

*"Come out of the masses. Stand alone like a lion and live your life according to your own light."*

– Osho

"So, are you going to Turkey on vacation?" Richard asked.

"Umm…well, both yes and no," Zoya said with a laugh, pulling her hair back and twisting it into a loose knot.

He looked at her inquiringly.

"An art gallery has commissioned me to work on a set of paintings. They are coming up with a coffee-table book on dance forms. So, I am on my way to Konya for the Mevlana Festival. Plus, I enjoy traveling. So this trip is going to be a good mix of business and pleasure. Two days in Istanbul and then off to Konya by morning flight," she said, her eyes lighting up. She suddenly looked like a young girl.

"Hmm. What's this festival about?"

"It's a Sufi celebration through dance. The whirling dervishes… I hope to capture their movement on canvas."

He looked at her blankly.

"Men dressed in white robes and tall hats, spinning in circles. Does that ring a bell?" she asked, sensing his confusion.

"Ah yes, it does! I think I saw it in a documentary," Richard replied.

"That dance is called the Sema," she explained.

"And what's Mevlana?"

"Mevlana means our master. So the Dervishes are known as the Mevlevi Order. Actually, they are followers of a Sufi mystic, Mevlana Jalāl ad-Dīn Muhammad Rūmī; hence the name. The order has been celebrating Rumi's death for almost 750 years, marking his 'wedding night' with God."

Richard was suddenly seized with a sense of the bizarre.

It was almost surreal. Sitting here and talking to this odd woman on topics that seemed strange, unreal even. Wedding night with God? "You have to be kidding", he muttered to himself. It was as if she had walked in from a parallel universe, twirling her hair, talking of things he had only vaguely heard of and discarded just as brusquely.

Life for him was simple, clear-cut, a well thought out path planted with ideas and concepts that were strong, rooted, visible and unarguable. And yet, he could think of many instances where he had been surprised by people who had defied all logic and had taken odd decisions. Once, when he had been grappling with a design problem for a tool, he was taken in by a strong urge to drink coffee at his favorite café. Though the coffee shop was four blocks away, he decided to take the break. It was peak time and all tables were occupied except for one by the door. Not too happy with the option, he decided to take it. Then, while pondering the problem, he noticed a pile of books lying on a shelf. It was as if somebody had walked by and toppled them. But the way they had fallen, struck him as odd. Suddenly, he realized he was staring the design change in the face. He rushed back to his factory and tried the same pattern. It worked! Everyone commended him for it. He tried hard to attribute the idea to random chance, but something in him told him it had been bigger than that.

"So, who's Rumi?" he asked, brushing back his hair consciously when he caught her looking at him. It was as if she had secretly wandered into his mind and was reading his thoughts.

"Rumi was a Sufi mystic from Persia. He was born somewhere between 1200 and 1207 AD. He started out as a scholar and came to be revered as a wise philosopher. He was very popular and had a large following," said Zoya, almost in awe. She was obviously quite impressed with this gentleman, Richard thought.

"And?"

"And? And there was still something missing in his life. He felt it too. But he didn't know what."

"So did he find what he was looking for?"

"Are you always this impatient?" she asked, squinting her eyes and peering at him closely. "I bet you are one of those guys who like to read the ending of the book first, to find out if it's worth all the trouble," she added.

"If I am, what's wrong with it? It's better than wasting time on a bad book," he said, shrugging his shoulders and looking away.

"Well, the good stuff, the juice, is right in the middle. Now tell me, what is more fun?" she asked, when she caught him sighing. "When you are right in the middle of enjoying a glorious mango, its wonderful heady flavors overwhelming your senses, or when you are done eating it hurriedly?"

But he did not look impressed.

"OK, so probably a mango is not familiar territory for you. Maybe, a double-grilled cheeseburger in your case."

"Thank you for your kind consideration. And by the way, it would be a steak, done medium rare, in my case. So if we are done with the mango homage, what happened next to Mr. Rumi?" asked Richard.

"He met Shams. Shams Tabrisi," she answered with a close-lipped smile.

She certainly took her time to reveal her stories, angling for his curiosity until it reached a peak and he gave in.

"Oh well, Shams was a wandering mystic who appeared almost out of nowhere. According to the story, he was in search of a companion who could be his kindred spirit, be a mirror to him," Zoya answered a little hurriedly when she caught him glaring.

"Actually, not much is known about Shams."

"What happened then?"

"In spite of coming from completely different backgrounds, Rumi – an elite, educated nobleman – and Shams – a poor wandering dervish – soon developed a deep friendship. They became inseparable. Rumi, who had so far related to God only in terms of concepts, rules and theories, was impressed with Shams, who saw God in everything. Shams forced Rumi to confront his boundaries, his beliefs. They spent long hours immersed in discussion and meditation. Shams brought alive Rumi's inner yearning for God. As the distance between them grew smaller, Rumi grew further apart from his world, his people," Zoya said.

She continued, "As it usually happens, their bond began to make Rumi's friends and followers jealous. Because of Shams, increasing proximity, they began to feel alienated and distant from Rumi. After sensing their discomfort, Shams even left Konya. But Rumi implored him to come back. One day, when they were together, Shams heard someone calling him outside. He went out the door but never came back.

"It is alleged that Rumi's followers killed Shams. That incident changed Rumi. He was never the same again. "

"Hmm, grief often does that," he mumbled.

"I guess because grief brings us towards a moment of singularity. A moment where everything as we know it, changes. You are left with nothing to hold on to except to understand what life is trying to teach us through the experience. We can either take its hand and climb out or turn away and sink in. It's a choice we make."

"So what happened to Rumi?"

"For Rumi, his redemption came through love. Through his love for Shams, Rumi finally found his calling. It was as if a gateway to the beyond had opened up. From a self-assured, accomplished master, he turned into a poet, a mystic and a lover; a madman lost in love. It was Shams, who had introduced Rumi to music and poetry. He began journeying inwards. Expressing himself through music and poetry was his way of connecting with the outside world. Over a span of 25 years right up to his death in 1275 AD, Rumi composed over 70,000 verses of poetry. And believe it or not, the verses make sense even to this day. They are timeless. Listen to this:

'The minute I heard my first love story,
I started looking for you, not knowing
how blind that was.
Lovers don't finally meet somewhere.
They're in each other all along.'

"Isn't that beautiful?" Zoya asked animatedly.

"Hmm, yeah it's good," Richard said. "So what's with the whirling? You still didn't explain that."

Zoya replied, "One day, when Rumi was wandering on the streets overcome with grief, he became engrossed in the rhythmic beat of a goldsmith's hammer and began to whirl to it. And as he kept on whirling, he entered into a kind of a meditative trance. Umm, how do I explain this? Okay, did you whirl as a child?"

"Uhh, yes, I did. I think all children do," he said.

"And how did that make you feel?"

"Well, you end up feeling a little funny in the head."

"That funny feeling in the head is what the Sufis are looking for," she said, laughing.

"What do you mean?" he asked.

"When you whirl, you see that along with your body, even the world around you is moving. Come to think of it, the entire cosmos is whirling. Right from our galaxies, to the planets, stars, atoms, electrons and protons – everything is involved in a cosmic dance. But there comes a point where, within all that movement, you sense a certain stillness. You sense the observer at the center, who is unmoving – that observer is you. It's as if you have become the quiet eye of the hurricane, a witness to the whirlwind around you."

"A witness?" he asked, leaning back in his chair, his brow furrowed.

"A witness to the truth of our existence. Everything is born out of this cosmos and everything returns to it," she explained. "When I was a kid, my mom always used to say when I'd reach out for a glass of water in a restaurant: 'Don't drink it. You don't know where this water has come from.' And she was right. Who knows where this drop of water has come from? Today, it forms part of my body. Tomorrow, when I die, it will return to the universe and probably form the tail end of a comet.

"And like that, we are all born of this existence and will return to it. Isn't that fact alone enough to awaken us to our intrinsic oneness?" she asked, raising her hands in wonder and smiling.

"Anyway, coming back to the Sema, that feeling of becoming a witness is what all who meditate, including the Sufis, aim for."

"Why is becoming the witness so important?" he asked.

"It's difficult to explain. It has to be experienced," she said, looking up thoughtfully.

She added, "Let's see. How would you like to be in a state where you can deal with everything with a sense of equanimity? While pain and happiness still have the power to move you, they do not affect your ability to respond with composure. Like watching a movie; viewing life from the outside in. You laugh, you cry, you even feel angry with the characters. But once you leave the theatre, you can drop the baggage because you know it is not real."

"So are you saying life is not real? Or there is no meaning to it?" he queried.

"It is real to the extent you think it is. It has meaning to the extent you create meaning in it. For example, what is this flower?" she asked, pointing to the small bouquet arranged in the middle of their table.

"If explained scientifically, it's just a collection of cells arranged in a particular symmetry that reflect the color red and give out a particular odor. But we see it as a fragrant red rose, a pristine symbol of love, of beauty, of adornment... so you see, it is *we* who give meaning to it," said Zoya.

"Beauty lies in the eyes of the beholder," Richard piped in.

"Precisely! Similarly, life is what we think it is. Once you realize this, you simply accept life as it is."

"Won't that distance you from life? Or make you rather disconnected from everybody else?" he asked.

"On the contrary, it will make you more compassionate, because then you will see the futility of judging yourself and others. There will be no need to attack or feel attacked. And since we are all part of the same cosmos, what's the point in running away? What can we escape from, anyway?"

"Well, but what about your opinions, beliefs, likes or dislikes?"

"You are the sole creator and owner of them. If you like something, and that makes sense to you, you accept it. If not, you ignore it. There is no need for somebody else to agree or validate your opinion. You are essentially free, once you realize it."

"Then how do we decide what's right or wrong for us?" he asked, probing deeper.

"Come to think of it, your feeling is your only true guide. Everything or everybody else can simply be channels to show us different paths, different expressions, but the decision to interpret and choose, rests with us. And like us, everybody else is on their own path and entitled to their own individual truth or meaning," she said.

"But if everyone believes in their own version of truth, won't they start to cross others' paths and run them down?" he countered.

"No, quite the contrary. Once you believe you have the freedom to pursue your own truth, you have to, by that same logic, give that latitude to everybody else as well. Coming to accept this fact alone would end more than half the conflicts in the world."

"Hmm, you have a point," he nodded slowly. "So are you a Sufi?"

"Well, I am on the path," she answered slowly.

"Hmm. So this trip, you are traveling alone?" he asked, with an air of casual indifference.

"Uh, yes," she answered firmly.

"Oh," he said sympathetically. But oddly enough, he didn't feel that way.

"Why 'oh'? While I don't argue against the pleasures of togetherness, sometimes it's good to travel alone. In fact, I think everyone should. You sample a lot more of life," she said with a determined nod.

"Hmm. How do you mean?" he asked.

"Well for starters, if I were here with someone, this seat wouldn't be empty. And we would never have had this conversation. And I would have never gotten the top secret insider's scoop on chassis development and its impact on the world automobile market," she whispered in mock seriousness.

They both began laughing.

"By the way, aren't you getting late for whatever you were getting late for?" she said, suddenly checking her watch.

"I guess I can take some more time away. I have the whole eight hours on the flight for work. So tell me, have you been to Turkey before?" he leaned forward, enthusiastically dousing a piece of *idli* with *sambar*, the yellow curry by the side of his potatoes.

## Bringing It to Life: Messages from Chapter Two – Attracting Positive Coincidences

### The Storyline

Richard and Zoya's meeting in the story seems like an accident but actually isn't. This chance meeting has begun to reveal itself to be much more than a mere coincidence. Something closer to providence is guiding change into both Richard and Zoya's life.

### Messages

*"Be grateful for whoever comes, because each has been sent as a guide from beyond."*

– Rumi

### Reflect on the following questions:

- Is your desire strong and noble?

- Is your desire consistent?

- Are your actions and desire aligned with each other?

- Do you notice and record coincidences in your life?

- Do you express gratitude for every coincidence or lucky break that helps you achieve your goals or has the potential to help you achieve your goals?

- Do you look at every coincidence, whether positive or

negative, as a chance incident that in some way propels you towards your goals?

• Do you regularly visualize and affirm your goals?

Like attracts like; we all invariably attract what we focus on. When your mind is actively fixed on a particular goal, you seem to be more attuned to people, information and activities related to it.

Have you noticed that when you're thinking about choosing a particular brand of car, you keep noticing that brand everywhere you go? Or if you are expecting a baby, you seem to see more pregnant women than you did before? Brian says in his seminars that you are a "living magnet", you invariably attract the right people, ideas and opportunities into your life that are harmonious with your goals.

When you focus on a goal, the reticular activating system (RAS), a part of your brain that functions as a filter to process over four hundred billion bits of information per second that you are exposed to every single day, searches for people, places and circumstances to support what you are thinking about. Simply put, if you have well-defined goals, RAS will direct your attention towards people, events and opportunities that can help achieve your aspirations.

According to the Quantum Mechanics theory in physics, 'The Observer Effect' refers to changes that the very act of observation will make on a phenomenon being observed. In a similar vein, each of us creates our own future through our thoughts. You can use this knowledge to be in command of your own existence and create coincidences in your life.

In his book, *SynchroDestiny*, Deepak Chopra used the famous Grinberg-Zylberbaum experiment (1987) to prove that we are all connected on a spiritual level. The experiment documented two meditating subjects who were able to feel mentally connected even when placed in separate rooms – when one was exposed to bright flashes of light, the other meditator's brain responded as if he too were being exposed to flashes of light.

This isn't just proven by lab studies. Many artists, thinkers, performers and creators were able to embark upon their careers because of serendipitous moments like these:

– Jazz musician James Morrison and his brother were trying to make it big in New York, but ended up playing music on the streets. They made enough money to get a burger from *Burger Boy*, and within hours of eating his burger, James was flying business class, eating smoked salmon on his way to Europe for a major jazz tour. It turned out that a waiter at *Burger Boy* spotted his trumpet and put the Morrisons in touch with an agent who urgently needed a replacement for a sick soloist.

– While Harrison Ford dabbled in acting in the 1960s, he also took up carpentry, earning more as a woodworker, than as an actor playing small parts in television shows. During that time, he accumulated mentors, one of whom eventually led him to director George Lucas, who chose him for a role in the 1973 film, *American Graffiti*. Luckily for Harrison, both Christopher Walken and Al Pacino turned Lucas down when presented with the role of Han Solo in the 1977 mega-hit, *Star Wars*.

– David Letterman, the late-night funny man, broke into the business with a flop. After a string of guest appearances on comedy shows, sitcoms and game shows, Letterman landed a hosting gig for a TV pilot called *The Riddlers*. The series was a bust, but Letterman got noticed by the producers of *The Tonight Show with Johnny Carson*. He soon became a regular guest, and eventually a TV talk show host who earned $40 million a year.

These are some examples of coincidences that may appear to be simply accidents. However, as Albert Einstein said: "Coincidence is God's way of remaining anonymous."

If you have never experienced positive coincidences, you may be wondering why. Here are a few reasons:

• You have goals but no burning desire to succeed. You do not put in enough effort to succeed. This gives the Universe mixed signals, indicating you are not sure if these are your true goals.

• Your desire is not consistent.

• Your action and desires are not aligned. There is scattered energy leading you away from your goals.

• You are not grateful for the good things that happen to you.

• You accomplish many things but don't acknowledge your successes. As a result, your goals do not lead to happiness and joy, thus reducing your energy to achieve them.

- You have desires but no awareness. You do not see the connection between your desires, actions and results. This causes inappropriate reactions and actions and eventually leads to missed results.

- You do not affirm and visualize your goals regularly.

Many of us fear the unplanned because we only see the possibility for negative outcomes or results. But even a negative outcome can ultimately lead us in the right direction. An unhappy experience in your life, such as being fired from work, can open new doors for you that lead to a new and better career. Overall, though, if you focus too much on bad experiences you will invite more of the same. But if you turn them into just another chapter in the narrative of success, you'll find it easier to draw positive solutions.

Azim did not enjoy his accounting job with Thorne Riddell, which at the time was one of the big eight accounting firms in the world. This led him to join a smaller firm where he thrived, becoming a partner, then managing partner, then branching out to several locations to eventually become an inspirational speaker and best-selling author. All this would never have happened if he had been successful with his first job.

Problems and setbacks come to everyone. In chapter thirteen, we share how Brian turned his early selling setbacks around to eventually becoming a sales guru.

Steve Jobs might have felt victimized after he was

fired from Apple. He chose to react differently. After his dismissal, he grasped crisis by the horns, seeing opportunity where others did not. He went on to lead a small animation company and turned it into the juggernaut that is now Pixar. When The Walt Disney Company bought Pixar in 2006, Jobs immediately became the largest shareholder in Disney. Moral of the story: when unwanted changes happen, look beyond them and see the opportunity they might contain.

*Challenge yourself with the following 'How to' exercises:*

1) BECOME more aware of what is going on in your life and start actively looking for coincidences. Once you do this, the power of coincidence will become more apparent to you.

2) RECORD all the coincidences you observe in a week. Analyze them to see how many of these directly or indirectly helped you to achieve your goals.

3) EXPRESS gratitude for every event that helps you achieve your goals or has the potential to help you achieve your goals.

4) SET clear goals yearly, quarterly, monthly, weekly. Read them every night before you go to sleep and every morning when you wake up. The clearer your goals, the more frequently coincidences occur to help you attain your goals.

5) ALIGN your goals with the purpose of helping others. The unseen help (coincidences) occurs more often because now you are a partner with the Universe. Therefore, ensure that your goals are not just selfish

but also selfless. When you want to help others, the Universe wants to help you.

6) TRUST that all coincidences (negative and positive) are there to help you, even though you may not think so at the time.

7) DURING each encounter (positive and negative) ask yourself: How does it help me achieve my goals, teach me something or bring greater awareness into my life?

8) WHEN you face obstacles in the way of your accomplishments, embrace them as positive coincidences rather than negative elements. Such an approach will help you achieve your goals in the end. Brian describes this as becoming an inverse paranoia – believe that there is great conspiracy in the universe to make you happy and successful, and everything that happens is a part of it.

If you have faith that the Universe is there to help you, you will find this concept easier to accept. What is important is that you are clear about your goals, and that you take action every day to achieve them. You then begin to look at every setback as a stepping stone toward your goals.

Chapter Three

# Creating Heightened Awareness

*"When you touch one thing with deep awareness, you touch everything."*

– Thich Nhat Hanh

They waited patiently in the slow-moving line to collect their boarding passes.

Business class was full and last-minute booking had ensured that Richard had to wait in a long line of people queuing for the economy class.

He eyed the short business class queue enviously – the passengers being cleared swiftly through the formalities.

Finally, it was his turn. He handed the ticket to a pretty, well-coiffured Indian girl with impeccably manicured nails. She checked it for a moment and said, "Sir, due to the delay in Delhi, our landing clearance at Istanbul has been delayed and we now will be stopping over in Dubai for three hours. So would you like to change this flight or carry on?"

"Damn! When is the next flight?"

"It's tomorrow at 9 am, sir."

"In that case, I will keep this booking," he sighed.

"Sir, your passport?"

He fumbled for his passport in his trouser pocket. But it was empty. He checked again, trying to remember the last time he had seen it.

"It's in your coat pocket," Zoya whispered from behind.

She was right. There it was.

"Thanks! How did you know?"

"You put it there when you were contemplating whether or not to reveal your top secret."

"Well, you are certainly not going to forgive me for that one, are you?" he asked, shaking his head.

They both laughed.

"Are you both together?" the girl at the counter asked.

"Uh, yeah, I guess so," he faltered and glanced behind.

"So can I give you seats together, then?" she continued.

"Sure!" Zoya answered with a smile.

Richard waited as Zoya completed her immigration formalities. After collecting their boarding passes, they walked together towards security check. The airport was crowded and they had to stop frequently to let others pass.

"You remembered about the passport. That's very observant of you," he said in admiration.

"I am generally observant of people and things around me. It's being aware at each moment that is a challenge." she replied.

"So has that something to do with being a Sufi?"

"As a matter of fact, yes. Awareness is the first and the most important step," she said.

"Really? Somehow I never connected divinity with being aware."

"Well, awareness simply means being awake. But awake with alertness, with a certain intensity, a totality. Have you ever watched a cat? Most of the time, it looks very relaxed. But it is always very alert and watchful. A small movement, a noise and immediately you can see its tail twitching. In fact, all animals are very alert. But we humans spend our lives as if we have been sleeping. We see without really seeing," she explained.

"How do you mean?"

"We go through life as if on autopilot. We have become so efficient at everything we do that we no longer need any awareness to live it. Unless we are hit by turbulence or a sudden big change, we become immune to our environment. We wake up, brush our teeth, get ready and drive to work. Sometimes we reach work and don't even remember the drive."

"Well, efficiency is good," he ventured.

"It is. But not when it makes you numb to life itself. I mean, just as we are on autopilot with our tasks, we are also on autopilot with our thoughts, our fears, our opinions. And that's where the danger lies. Have you noticed that many of our fears are so old? And most of them are not even our own. They are borrowed – from our parents, society and friends. They have stuck around because we have accepted them blindly, on autopilot, without even examining them. The rest of the time, we are either thinking about the past or worrying about the future. So our mind is never really in the present."

"Why not? I am with you right now, in the present."

"Yes, but the moment you start thinking about being with me here, you have already left the present and are now in the past. The more we spend time in defining things, the more unconscious we are of the present moment. This moment is the source of our present happiness and also the origin of the future we can create."

"For example, I'll never be this old again after today; in fact, after this very moment. And all the time I spend living in my past or worrying about the future, I waste the tremendous possibilities that lie within these moments."

"That's a wonderful way to express it. It really brings forth the urgency of each moment," he added.

"It does, doesn't it? You know, recently I went on a trek with a group. Personally, I am a little scared of heights. In fact, little might be an understatement," she winked.

"But the organizer assured me the trek was not a dangerous one. So off we went on our trail, eating chocolates and peanuts. But gradually, the trail started to narrow down and as we went higher, we encountered more and more snow. Towards the last leg of our trip, we discovered the road up the mountain was covered in snow. And the path, which was at least 5 feet wide earlier, had tapered down to only one foot wide.

"Anyway, the trek guide urged me to keep going. At first, the excitement of coming this far egged me on. But as we continued the climb, it became more and more difficult. Nevertheless, we finally reached the top, and a breathtaking view of snow-covered peaks stood before us.

"We celebrated with a little fancy lunch and hot ginger lemon tea. But the climb down was an altogether different experience. The snow had now melted in the afternoon sun and become slippery. There was hardly any road in some patches. Add to that, my mortal fear of heights.

"So here I was with a fancy pair of sport shoes totally unsuited for this terrain, a narrow band of slippery ice and a deep ravine on one side. That hour of the precarious climb down was one of the most intense periods of my life. I crawled like an insect, on all fours, trying to grasp whatever I could. Till date, there are only three things I remember distinctly about that walk down: the wild beating of my heart, the butt of the trek guide and the two feet of snow in front of me," Zoya said.

"The butt of the trek guide?" asked Richard, laughing.

"Oh yes! As long as I saw his butt, I knew there was a road ahead," Zoya answered.

"So that was one of my best experiments in pure unadulterated awareness. The danger of that moment was so intense that I could not afford to walk in autopilot anymore. There were no other thoughts except about feeling my feet on the ground and taking the next step. I had to be constantly alert. One slip and everything would have been over in a second. That is how life is. Each moment is alive with possibility," she concluded.

"And for a Sufi, awareness would go a step further. They are not only alive to everything around them, but also conscious of the divine in everything. The trees, the water, the mountains, you, me, that little spider crawling on the wall ahead – everything is a reflection of the divine. So the first and most important step is cultivating awareness. Be aware of every little act you do. Be aware of each thought, emotion, feeling that you experience. Let everything around you and within you become an opportunity for you to be aware," she explained.

"That's a pretty tall order," he countered.

"Well, I assure you that if you take care of this order, you can have pretty much anything on the menu," she replied with a small bow.

"Even in business. For example, I recently read about a pizza joint that launched 'oven delivery': pizzas being cooked even as they are being delivered. Electric ovens were installed on the back of motorcycles to reduce delivery time and improve quality of the pizza. Come to think of it, there are endless possibilities for growth if only we are alert to life. Try it, if you don't believe me," she leaned forward and whispered.

"And that brings us to our security check where we must part ways, to meet again. See you on the flight!" And with that, Zoya walked across to the women's line.

He tried it then. He tried to be aware of everything that was happening around him.

He saw that the security officer smiled at him while asking for his jacket. Normally, he would have missed it. But this time he smiled back. He watched a toddler in a bright red sweater throwing a tantrum and his mother trying her best to appear in control while dragging her grey striped bag. He suddenly remembered a childhood memory of his mom dragging in a big bucket of washing every Saturday, while he would run around her, trying to draw her attention. He became aware of a rush of warmth in his throat as the mother finally gave up the bag and picked up the child, patting him gently and murmuring in his ear.

He then noticed a newlywed Indian wife walking timidly behind her husband, who appeared even more timid than the wife. It was probably their first international trip. Richard smiled when the wife crept forward and clutched her husband's hand, who then visibly relaxed. He noticed the rush of people striding around him purposefully but going nowhere in particular, busy with their phones; sampling stuff vacantly at airport shops, waiting for time to pass. He became aware of himself checking his watch, almost as a reflex, but not really noticing the time. He headed for a chair, sat down and carefully put his boarding pass in his coat pocket.

And then he became aware of something else.

With the very act of watching, he seemed to have better clarity. The more watchful he became, the more deliberate and unhurried were his movements. Everything he did acquired a certain meaning, a rhythm. Simultaneously, he realized that the constant chatter of thoughts in his head quietened a little. He felt visibly lighter. However, the moment he became aware of this process, he lost touch with the awareness of *that* moment. It was a tricky road, this path of awareness. It was as if he was watching a movie in which he was the main protagonist. No, it was not that either… because he could watch his own feelings, his own wonder... so what was it then?

He shook his head. This was going a little too far. But she was right – awareness did bring everything to life! It could even help you be more open, separate opportunities from problems, Richard said to himself.

He remembered his last board meeting. The presentation had been splendid. Everyone seemed to be impressed and was making all the right noises. Yet the next day, the board members had somehow changed their minds and declined to give their consent.

He went over that evening once again, carefully playing back each moment. Then it dawned on him that there was one member who had not looked at him during the entire presentation – Mr. Goodman. He was a quiet, reticent man in his seventies with a paunch, a wheezing cough and generally not much of an opinion.

In fact, he had looked away whenever Richard had tried to make eye contact. Later on, Richard had seen him mumble something under his breath to another member.

But Richard had not paid attention to it because he was exulting in the supposed success of a great presentation. Now, looking back, he felt being aware of Mr. Goodman's remoteness would have given him a cue as to the board's decision.

*So she was right*, thought Richard. *Ultimately, awareness was in fact the precursor, the kernel from which everything emerged, or was rather revealed. Without awareness, we would continue to remain in a bubble, oblivious to life changing and evolving every moment, around us and in us.*

Richard looked around vacantly, and realized that he was actually looking for Zoya. He spotted her at a bookstore at the far end of the airport. She seemed to be making a purchase and, not surprisingly, was engrossed in an animated conversation with the cashier who was smiling shyly.

Richard smiled a little. *Yes*, he thought, *she had the ability to draw people with her warmth and surprise them with her genuineness.*

# Bringing It to Life: Messages from Chapter Three – Creating Heightened Awareness

### *The Storyline*

Cultivating awareness can help us experience life more fully. Zoya illustrates this by noticing where Richard put his passport, and such attentiveness can allow us to understand the world around us – and its reactions to us – at a deeper level.

### *Messages*

*"You are the sky. The clouds are what happens, what comes and goes."*

– Eckhart Tolle

### *Reflect on the following questions:*

- What bothers you the most?

- What excites you?

- What do you do well?

- What can you do better?

- What makes you happy?

- What does success mean to you?

- Do you write a regular journal to increase your awareness?

- Do you actively listen or simply wait for the other person to finish before you speak?

- Are you up to date with what is happening in your field?

- Are you and your team crystal clear about your vision, mission, values and strategy?

- Do you communicate effectively?

Hundreds of thoughts go through one's mind at any given time. Your work may be challenging, or you have been fired, or you are facing problems in a relationship. These thoughts often have no particular direction. You need to rise above your thoughts, to become the 'sky' in the metaphor. That way, you become the objective listener to your thoughts. This sets you on the path of self-awareness.

Awareness is the starting point of every quest. Without awareness, we flounder along the path. Awareness removes digressions and shows a clear path ahead.

Once you are sorted in your mind about your purpose in life, the next step is to define the roadmap to attain your goal. Of course, there will be changes as you go along, but having a broad framework of a plan is essential. Excellent communicators and transformational leaders are focused and clear about their direction and purpose.

What you seek is seeking you all the time, even though you do not realize it. This is how the Universe is designed. You invite this unseen help when your desire is consistent and your awareness is relaxed and clear.

Awareness means achieving greater clarity and honesty in all aspects of your life. You understand what others are trying to communicate to you at a deeper and more realistic level. You're able to be honest with yourself about your faults and your positive traits, and you have a greater ability to lead. The benefits of heightened awareness include accepting that we are responsible for our actions, expectations and beliefs and how they influence what we do. It helps us notice our patterns (good and bad) and work towards channelizing our negative emotions into constructive actions.

People often judge others, yet most people don't really know themselves. It is difficult to know yourself, and almost impossible to know another person completely. This is why so many people are intent on judging others – they're afraid to learn about themselves. Aristotle has thus rightly said: "To know thyself is the highest wisdom."

Heightening awareness can seem like a tall order for those of us who block out the world in order to focus on their own life. But heightened awareness won't take your attention away from the necessary tasks in your life. On the contrary, there is a huge upside to this in terms of progress in the corporate world, and you getting more respect from your colleagues, clients and family.

Writing a journal regularly, is a great awareness builder. There is no one particular way to do this. The key is to write what suits you. It can be as little as jotting down a few bullet points before you go to bed. Ask yourself: What did I learn about myself at work today? What did I learn at home? What made me happy and what made me unhappy today and why? What are my goals?

Greater awareness also helps us differentiate between reality and wishful thinking. Many people lead an illusionary life (a life built on how you wish things would be, but not how they are), which prevents them from getting to the root of problems. As a result, they fail to deliver. For example, when you get angry with another driver, you believe your anger has been triggered by his poor driving. But in reality, you are stressed out because you have missed the deadline for an important project. Awareness allows you to be mindful of what is really going on and why you are reacting the way you are.

Awareness is also achieved through active listening – listening with your eyes, ears and heart. Give your undivided attention and remain non-judgmental. Many people listen only with their ears. They miss out on body language, which constitutes much of the communication. Your relationship with your family can be tenuous without active listening because a deep understanding of each other is missing. The same applies to business relationships, be it with customers, colleagues or other stakeholders. If you practice active listening, you can enrich every relationship in your life.

In the corporate world, being aware of the moods of individuals and teams can offer valuable insights. You need to know if your employees feel valued or demotivated. Heightened awareness helps you fix situations where your employees may feel less than great.

Awareness also means you have a deeper understanding of what is going on in your business. You are aware of what is most important to you. Many entrepreneurs, surprisingly, are not very clear about what they need to focus more on.

Being aware means not only that you are clear about your vision, mission, values and strategy, but also whether your team and your actions are aligned with them.

### Challenge yourself with the following 'How to' exercises:

1) ACCEPT that your awareness can always be enhanced.

2) ASK yourself: What frustrates me? What bothers me? What excites me? What do I do well? What can I do better? What does success mean to me? What makes me happy? What takes me away from who I am?

3) HAVE one-to-one meetings with associates, customers, family members, colleagues and your spouse to find out how they're feeling. Keep an open mind during discussions about issues and relationships and listen actively (with eyes, ears and heart). When you're feeling upset about something, ask the question: what else could it be?

4) SHARPEN your awareness of team members you work with: are they performing to the best of their abilities? What are the gaps between actual outcome vis-à-vis expected outcome? Who are the performers/ non-performers? What will take them to the next level?

   You can use the Myers-Briggs Type Indicator (or MBTI), which is useful for understanding preferences for interacting with others. Psychometric Tests are also useful for helping people understand their personality traits; get an objective view of how they behave, and how they compare in outlook with others.

5) DEEPEN your awareness of your business. Evaluate what is being achieved from a qualitative and quantitative standpoint, and have a mechanism for evaluation. Then determine the one thing you can do which gives you the highest leverage on your time and results, and focus on it. Set weekly, monthly, quarterly and yearly goals and evaluate your quantitative and qualitative progress regularly.

6) DEVELOP a deeper awareness of your offerings: What are their strengths and weaknesses? Which products and services do clients really like and which do not add much value? The exercise described in point number 5 helps here too.

7) BE AWARE of your customer mix: Who are the 20 percent customers giving you 80 percent of the business? Focus more on them.

8) As noted earlier, WRITE in a journal – about what's going on in your life, business and family – to get to the root of any problem. Writing has the power to unclutter the mind. Write in a journal before addressing a problem directly with the person concerned, or read your journal before going for an important meeting. Soon after you begin writing, you'll find that you're more aware of your behavior, your business and people around you. If you are worried about having to

invest a lot of time, or going blank while writing, fear not. Invest as little as 5 to 10 minutes a day to write as few as two or three bullet points.

# Chapter Four

# Being Content in the Present Moment

*"Always say 'yes' to the present moment... surrender to what is. Say 'yes' to life and see how it suddenly starts working for you rather than against you."*

*– Eckhart Tolle*

"So what did you buy?" Richard asked. They were now seated and the flight attendant was giving pre-flight safety instructions to passengers.

"So somebody was watching?" said Zoya, raising her eyebrows and smiling.

"Well it comes with the territory of 'being aware'," he nodded sagely, with an air of mock self-importance.

"It's a book, *The Zen of Creativity: Cultivating Your Artistic Life*. So tell me, how was your experiment in being aware?" she asked, turning towards him.

"Well, it was quite interesting. It's not that I have never sensed this feeling of awareness; it's just a more tangible acknowledgement of that feeling now. But it's very easy to slip into your thoughts again. So you have to be watchful," he explained, somehow feeling dissatisfied with his account.

"It gets better with practice," she said.

"I can see that," he replied with a quick nod.

"You know there is a nice Zen anecdote about this."

"Well from Sufism to Zen philosophy. Interesting!" he exclaimed with a hint of incredulity.

"Well, everything is connected at the core. The perennial philosophies across the world, irrespective of their origin, essentially talk about the same things. So anyway, about the story: there was a Zen disciple named Tenno. After ten years of rigorous training, he qualified as a teacher of Zen philosophy. One rainy morning, he went to meet the famous Zen master, Nan-in. When he walked in, the master greeted him with a question, 'Did you leave your wooden clogs and umbrella on the porch?'

"'Yes,' Tenno replied. 'Tell me,' the master continued, 'Did you place your umbrella to the left of your shoes or to the right?'

"Tenno did not know the answer, and realized that he had not yet attained full awareness. So it's not about remembering where you kept the umbrella or the passport, it's about being aware *in* and *of* each moment," Zoya explained.

"Hmm, you are right. We might be missing so much that happens each moment because we are so caught up in our thoughts. Over and above everything, we are missing life itself," he said.

"And the takeoff!" she suddenly piped in.

"Excuse me?" he asked.

She was sitting back in her chair, her hands gripping the armrest and keeping her eyes tightly shut.

"Oh pardon me! But I love takeoffs and landings. I think it has something to do with my fear of heights. I simply find the whole process very thrilling and terrifying all at the same time," she explained, her eyes still shut.

The plane hurtled down the runway, speeding across the tarmac towards the sky.

"There, did you feel it?" she asked him, looking gleeful.

"Feel what?" he asked with a laugh, finding her excitement amusing.

"The moment when the plane lifts off the ground. I mean, one moment you are rooted to the earth and the very next, you are weightless. And imagine this huge monstrosity flying with such incredible lightness in the air. It's like watching an elephant fly. Isn't it simply wonderful? The incredible lightness of being, hmm?" she asked happily.

"Well, actually it's a very simple law of physics, that when–," he started to explain but she cut him short.

"Oh I know this can be explained by science," she said, "but the wonder of flying is still so captivating."

"Yes, it is." He smiled both at her and her sense of wonder.

"So what's this book about?" he asked, seeing her tear the plastic wrap.

"Well, it's about how to rouse your creative spark, how to harness it at will, instead of waiting for your next creative breakthrough," she replied, peeling off the wrapping.

"So do you think you can become creative by reading books?" he asked, curious to know her point of view. He was sure by now that she would definitely add a whole new spin to it.

"Oh, you don't have to become what you already are. All of us are born creative. Every single one of us," she answered, waving her arm dismissively in the air.

"You think so?"

"I know so," she said, nodding sagely with a smile.

"Interesting! So how do you define creativity?" he asked.

"Umm… to me, creativity means loving whatever you do. Enjoying the act, whatever it is, celebrating it, reveling in it, losing yourself in it," she answered with a winsome smile.

"I don't think many people believe they are creative. In fact, one of the major challenges I face with my team is their restrictive thinking. Very few can think out of the box," he countered.

"That's because people have a limited idea about creativity. They think that if you can't paint, write, sculpt, dance or sing, you are not creative. But that's not true. Each one of us must explore what we can or cannot do."

Just then, the flight attendant interrupted them with refreshments. She was a petite girl in her early twenties, with eager eyes and a warm smile.

Richard opted for tea.

Zoya asked for an apple juice and then suddenly seemed to remember something and gestured to the attendant.

"Do you still offer those peanuts? Those Indian spicy ones?"

"Oh yes ma'am, we do," the air hostess replied politely, and handed Zoya a packet of peanuts along with the apple juice.

"I love the brand of peanuts they offer on this flight. Just the right amount of spice and crackle in the roast," Zoya explained.

The stewardess then carefully prepared Richard's tea. She tore open the tea bag package with one clean sweep and put a bag in the cup. She then gently poured hot water, careful not to spill any.

"Milk?"

"Yes please."

She poured just a little milk and stirred the tea gently, again taking care not to spill any. "Is that all, sir?" the air hostess confirmed.

"Yes. Thank you," Richard answered her with a smile.

Once she was gone, Zoya looked for a long moment in her direction and smiled.

"Did you see how beautifully she prepared your tea? So graceful. Almost as if she were painting a beautiful monsoon cloud," she answered, turning towards Richard.

"Where did that come from?" he asked with a smile.

"Nothing. I just feel creativity has nothing to do with any particular work. It has to do with the quality of awareness you bring to the act. Whether you are writing a novel or preparing tea, both can be creative. As long as you do it with love, grace and gratitude," she said softly.

"But if you do something simply as a duty, then that same act becomes a liability, a mundane activity that you will have to carry on your shoulders, no matter what," she added.

"But many of us grow up being conditioned to think that we are not creative. If a child is not painting masterpieces or composing like Beethoven, his parents tell him that he is not creative. And once a child begins to believe that he is not creative, he simply shuts down all possibilities," Richard observed, thinking of his own childhood, when he was continually told to achieve better grades, to make a better life to the exclusion of everything else. In fact, he couldn't recall his parents ever saying the word, 'creative'.

"Hmm, beliefs are very powerful. Instead of telling a child that he is not creative, he should be encouraged to explore and find his calling. Sometimes, it may take a lot of time, but it is totally worth it. And more often than not, during the quest, something wonderful begins to grow in the child," Zoya said.

"Yes, but I think parents are under a lot of pressure to help their children find good jobs, earn a living, make a lot of money," he answered.

"Well, if earning money is the key consideration, I think they are on the right path. But at what cost?" she asked, the color slowly rising in her cheeks as she continued.

"Being saddled with a job that pays well but is slowly killing you inside? So that by the time you are 40, you are nursing a paunch and are thoroughly bored of life? You reach a point where life starts to look like an endless and passionless march towards death. And as if that's not enough, you are also raising the next generation of emotionless souls. All our drinking, smoking, drugs and our mid-life crises are cries for help from this colorless existence. Life is essentially about finding some joy, some beauty and some absolution. Because humankind, by its very nature, is a potentiality, a work in progress."

"You seem to have a very high opinion of this world," he said.

"Well, I don't know about the world, but I certainly think highly of the individual. I believe each one of us is born with a destiny. We all have something to fulfill, some meaning to convey to the world. Existence never creates anything mindlessly, like a factory production. Every life is unique because existence intends to do something through it, for it," she added, her voice now steadily rising.

"You are really passionate about this subject," he exclaimed, his voice tinged with admiration.

"I am. Because every day I see so many people searching for purpose in their lives. But they never realize that life in itself has no meaning. It is we who have to create meaning out of life. Your life is your canvas. Only you can paint it, only you can express your potential. And we all are blessed with the freedom to do it," she added.

"I think people are scared. What if the search does not reveal anything? What if you come back empty-handed?" he replied.

"Tell me something. Why did you choose this particular profession? How did you start?" she asked.

"To be honest, my motives were not very different from those of others in this world. I wanted to make a lot of money, very fast," he replied, a little sheepishly.

"But still, there must have been something that pushed you towards this particular field of work," she persisted.

"Well, as a child I was fascinated with machines. I loved dismantling stuff. So while I was still studying engineering, I started my internship with a small factory next to my university. Within six months, I had studied the workings of most of the machines there. Many of these were very expensive back then and were imported.

"Within a year, I was repairing a few of them. Then I figured if you can take them apart, you can also put them together. I built my first machine with a budget of just $5,000 borrowed from a friend. I used that machine to set up a small workshop for motorbikes. From then on, it started to take on a life of its own.

"Within three years I was supplying components to an original equipment manufacturer. After a couple of years, when they decided to integrate backwards, they proposed to buy my company and offered me a position as senior manager on their design team. I saw this as an opportunity to work with bigger and better machines. And well, I never looked back after that.

"So, I guess my passion for engineering started it all," he concluded with a smile.

"So you took a leap of faith with that machine."

"I guess you can say that. She was my first," he replied.

They both laughed.

"You didn't have any idea where you would end up?" she asked.

"I didn't at that time," he answered, shaking his head.

"Well that's the point I'm making. You cannot live life if you are scared of coming back empty-handed. Yes, you can be safe. But if we are always concerned about safety, then inviting mediocrity is part of the protocol because when you want to be safe, you stop exploring new ideas or taking chances in life. You stick to the well-beaten path and, in the process, stop growing. I think mediocrity and safety are bosom pals," she replied.

"Yes, but many people are not sure what their true calling is. For me it was engineering design, so I guess I had it easy," said Richard.

"Actually, I feel that the less sure you are, the better. That way you get to experiment with a lot more than you'd imagine. Even if you think you know, you should not give up any chance to experience as many things as possible.

"The essence is that your search should be pure and unbiased. It's best not to begin with any pre-meditated conclusions, because then you are not searching, you are merely creating a framework to fit your opinions. You have to allow yourself to be open to inspiration," Zoya said.

"So where do you find your inspiration?" he asked.

"Umm... it's difficult to pinpoint exactly. Sometimes in the colors of the evening sky, or in the turn of a fresh leaf, somebody's quirky outfit, and even a child's laughter," she said, gazing with a faraway look in her eyes.

"A child's laughter?"

"Well, everything, even sounds or feelings, can be expressed visually. In fact, our senses are not static silos; they overlap, mix with each other. Someone might compose a tune looking at a sunrise. But I think inspiration is only the first step; the important part comes after that," she explained.

"And what's that?" he asked.

"Letting your inspiration take root in you. I agree that sometimes you are so enthused by your feelings that you have to immediately put it on paper. But mostly for me, it builds up to a heady crescendo slowly and steadily, and then becomes such a raging inferno that it has to find an outlet," she answered, bubbling with excitement.

"You are right. Sometimes, I see a pattern or a new product, or read something that captures my attention, and then forget all about it. A month later, suddenly, I feel that pattern welling up in me, at the most unexpected moments. It's almost surreal at times. It's like it was biding its time, waiting to strike just when I needed it the most," he added.

"Well that's the beauty of your inner being. It misses nothing," she said.

# Bringing It to Life: Messages from Chapter Four – Being Content in the Present Moment

### The Storyline

Zoya's enthusiasm for both Zen and Sufi philosophy is rooted in their approach to being in the present moment.

### Messages

*"Life is what happens to you while you're busy making other plans."*

– John Lennon

### Reflect on the following questions:

- Are you enjoying the ride to wherever you are going?

- Do you usually focus whole-heartedly on important things or get distracted?

- Do you allow interruptions in the day? If so, how can you prevent them?

- Are you often in a fire-fighting mode?

- Do you worry about petty things?

- Do you regularly count your blessings?

- Do you worry about what others think of you instead of focusing on doing your best?

All of us carry baggage from the past and are preoccupied with the future, which distracts us from the present moment. Many of our problems stem from this preoccupation, which causes low productivity, more stress, and less energy. It also substantially diminishes our capacity to understand, decide, recall and memorize, and also inhibits our ideas and creativity.

Studies show that people who multi-task or have high-profile, risk-taking jobs that involve crucial decision-making are less effective at their work, as compared to those who focus on one task at a time. Attention requires mental and physical energy that your body can create only in limited amounts. Focusing on anything consumes a considerable amount of glucose from your body and brain. This means distractions take both mental and physical toll on us.

Research also indicates that distractions take up almost two hours a day for most employees, most of whom only spend 11 minutes working on a project before they become distracted by something else, after which it takes them 25 minutes to refocus. So, in addition to affecting you at a personal level, distractions also have an adverse impact on your daily business targets.

You have a limited amount of energy, especially for tasks that are not uplifting or relevant. Therefore, whenever you engage in less important tasks, you deplete your energy.

Why do we get so distracted? Well, aside from distractions created by others, most of us become distracted by thinking about the past, the future… any time but the present.

When you are in the present moment, you're able to

powerfully engage with those around you. For instance, when Azim visits his 86-year-old father at his care home, he experiences two kinds of visits: In one, he is totally in the present moment with his father and there are no distractions. During these visits, they sit near a window overlooking a school and watch children play; this leads to deeper connections between the two. In the other kind of visit, Azim is distracted by phone calls and emails, or his father is called upon by care givers. At such times, there is little bonding. In fact, a shorter distraction-free visit is far more powerful than a longer visit fraught with interruptions.

This kind of power, which comes from focused interaction, can be applied to both your personal and professional life.

Similarly, in a business setting, when you meet your team, you can have two different types of meetings: one is where you are alert and open to both the verbal and non-verbal cues of your team, which helps you gather critical information to decide the next course of action. The other is where you have already made up your mind, and the meeting is held merely to manipulate others to accept your point of view; hence, you receive no valuable feedback from team members, which leads to sub-par performance.

*Challenge yourself with the following 'How to' exercises:*

1) EVERY hour, stop and ask: Am I really present in this moment? If not, what are my thoughts focused on? Doing this often will help you return to the present moment.

You may wonder how to practice this if you are

already doing an activity that is very engaging. Taking a moment to reflect on these questions will help you assess if you are really present and focused on the priority task– which is good – or if you are focused on a less important task.

2) SPEND a few minutes each day with Nature; it will calm you. Watch a tree's leaves move when the wind blows, reflecting non-resistance. While looking at the ocean, see the abundance, neutrality and oneness of the Universe. Nature has many messages for us and this practice will help separate your good thoughts from the cluttered ones. Spending some quiet time alone each day is essential to your inner well-being.

3) WHEN IN THE MOMENT, look at difficulties you have and ask: "What can I learn from this problem?" How is this problem affecting you in the larger scheme of things? Think about one thing you can do to minimize the problem and act upon it right away.

   Why this approach? Because it takes you away from the problem. Instead, you can start to act on the problem, which will help minimize the mental energy you invest in it and also create a realistic perspective on the situation.

4) ASK yourself: "What can I do in the present moment to create a positive impact?

5) SAY thank you a few times in a day for all the good things in your life. As you count your blessings, they multiply.

6) WHEN driving, observe your surroundings, listen to

music or an educational audio to stay in the present moment and avoid worrying about the serpentine traffic.

7) FORGIVE someone in the present moment by giving him the benefit of the doubt. This is liberating! Start with small things, such as when someone does not thank you for a favor you did, or when someone fails to apologize when they accidentally push you. As you get good at this, you will realize how much negative energy you stave off. This will help you forgive bigger transgressions, such as pardoning someone for taking away some of your business or cheating you on an investment deal.

8) THINK of someone you care about and send loving thoughts in the present moment.

# Chapter Five

# Practicing the Power of Meditation

*"Sometimes, simply by sitting, the soul collects wisdom."*

– Zen proverb

"Is there a way to connect better to one's inner being?" Richard asked Zoya.

"You can! Start meditating every day. It will help you bridge the gap between your outer and inner self. Once you start feeling more complete, you automatically start being present."

"Well, I have considered meditation, but the apparent pointlessness of simply sitting and doing nothing turns me off. I feel as if I'm wasting my time," he said.

"But why do you think everything has to have a point? Isn't your life already consumed with making so many points? Meditation is your opportunity to do nothing. No action, no thought, no emotion. You simply have to watch yourself. On a lighter vein, the good thing about meditation is that it makes "doing nothing" seem quite respectable," she chuckled.

"And eventually, even if your mind is absolutely quiet for one moment, that counts as meditation," she explained.

"So, it's like sleeping?" he asked.

"Well, if you can be watchful and alert while sleeping, then yes, it is sort of like sleeping," said Zoya, adding, "It's like I said before, being a watcher."

"The eye of the hurricane!" he exclaimed.

"You are right! Just like the eye of the hurricane, whose center is always calm despite the frenzied winds around it, your inner self too should be still and balanced irrespective of your circumstances," she replied with a smile.

"So, how do you go about it?"

Richard suddenly realized that he was enjoying himself.

Contrary to his first impressions, Zoya had turned out to be quite fascinating: a little strange, but interesting all the same. He also found that he enjoyed watching her talk, her large expressive eyes, and her animated gestures. Everything about her had a quality of wonder to it.

"Actually, there are many ways to approach meditation," she replied, and continued, "You should select the one that suits you best. Even going for a run can be meditative. The only rule is you have to be totally involved in whatever you are doing. So for many, the easiest way is to simply sit in a nice quiet corner and try to observe yourself. There are three key steps: First, start becoming aware of your body. Become aware of every movement. The easiest is to start with the breath. Once you start becoming aware of it, many unconscious or non-essential movements start to fade. The focus on breathing helps you feel connected to your body, diverting your attention from the incessant chatter of your thoughts and calming your mind.

"Yes, I did notice that," he nodded.

"Second, become aware of your thoughts. That's the slippery part. It's very easy to run away with a thought. For example, here you are watching that gentleman in the seat ahead eating chips and the very next moment, you start thinking about what you are going to have for lunch and from there on, one thought leads to another, and very soon you are thinking about your weight, your workout schedule, and it just goes on and on. And then suddenly you realize, wait a minute, I was watching that man…" she replied.

"And what's the third step?" he asked.

"Hold on, sparky!" she said with a laugh, "I am getting

there! The third is about watching your feelings. This step is even more complicated than the first two, because feelings are more subtle than thoughts. You don't even realize when one has slowly crept up, changing your state of mind in an instant. In fact, sometimes I wonder if feelings follow thoughts or thoughts follow feelings. Anyway, once you become aware of all these three levels, you are pretty much on your way," she said, raising her hand up.

"Way to?"

"Well, now that can only be experienced…" she sighed.

"Hmm, but if you had to explain it, what would you say?" asked Richard.

"Not everything in life can be explained. Some things can only be felt, like falling in love. Can you ever describe how *falling in love* feels? I mean you can give numerous platitudes, compose poetry, but you will still come nowhere close to explaining it. The other person will have to experience it to know it. But I guarantee, it's worth it," she answered with a resolute nod.

"What, falling in love or meditation?" he asked playfully.

"Both!" she replied, smiling gently.

"So you think people can become happier if they meditate?"

"Well, it can lead to bliss. And bliss is a state of mind that goes way beyond happiness," Zoya replied.

"So how do you know if you are close to reaching that state of bliss?" he asked.

"The point to remember here is that you have to become a watcher. As you go on watching, you start becoming more centered. Then gradually, another change begins to happen, this time from within you. The things you were watching begin to fade away as well, till you are left with a growing awareness of being watched; because watching implies a certain distance between the watcher and the watched. For example, if you stand too close to a picture, you will not be able to see it. Similarly, once you start watching your thoughts, you become detached from them. And because of this distance, they start losing their power to control you. As they lose power, thoughts start dropping off like flies, till you begin to experience brief but perceptible moments where you have no thoughts. This does not mean that you cannot use your mind. It simply means your mind cannot use you now. You become the master once again. And if you go deeper, you start to wonder *'who is the one watching that thought?'*

"In other words, who is watching the watcher? So eventually, the watcher becomes the watched. And that is when you merge into the whole. Your duality, your sense of separation from the rest of the world just melts away. You become the 'awakened'," she said softly.

"But like I said, you have to experience it to understand it," she added.

"So, have you?" Richard asked.

"Not yet. But the benefits on the path to attaining this state are so many that you increasingly feel inclined to continue the practice," she said.

"For instance, earlier, I couldn't separate myself from my emotions. Instead of analyzing them objectively, I would simply let myself be affected by them. If somebody said something hurtful to me, I would spend the rest of the day moping about it. But now I know that I am not my emotions.

"Meditation has helped me detach myself from my emotions and view them objectively. There are still many things that annoy me and I am unable to be objective about them. But now, when I give in to them, I know that I am not being true to myself. In other words, I can see my stupidity way better now," she said, concluding with a laugh.

There was a long silence, as Richard continued to watch her.

Zoya finally averted her eyes, a little self-consciously, and broke the silence, "So?"

"So, I think it's time I got back to my reports. I would like to complete them before we land in Dubai," Richard said, stretching and yawning.

"And I shall get back to my new book and hopefully get a little more creative before we land," she retorted.

# Bringing It to Life: Messages from Chapter Five – Practicing the Power of Meditation

## *The Storyline*

Richard and Zoya discuss meditation as a practice to help enhance awareness. She talks about watching the body, thoughts and feelings.

## *Messages*

Buddha was asked: "What have you gained from meditation?" He replied: "Nothing." "However", Buddha said, "let me tell you what I lost: Anger, Anxiety, Depression, Insecurity, Fear of Old Age and Death."

## *Reflect on the following questions:*

- Do you meditate regularly?

- Do you practice the power of meditation in all walks of life, including business?

- Are you able to focus on a task consistently, without distraction?

- Do you feel stressed out and negative?

- Are your activities aligned with your spirit?

- Do you set aside time for contemplation and reflection?

Meditation is an extremely effective tool to unleash the powers of concentration and bolster our inner strength. It can help us better manage our emotions, enabling us to respond to every situation with our totality of spirit and action.

Meditation – once thought of as a far out Eastern thing – is now considered a helpful habit practiced by successful people to develop better careers and lives. For example, the cofounders of Twitter, Google and Facebook all offer employees instruction in contemplative practices.

Meditation has become such a common element of business training that more than a thousand Googlers attended a training program called, *Search Inside Yourself*. Google even hosts bimonthly silent 'mindful lunches', which began after Zen monk and writer, Thich Nhat Hanh, visited Google in 2011.

Oprah Winfrey is also a strong believer in meditation, and gives her staff at Harpo Productions the opportunity to learn to meditate.

Why has meditation become so popular among business leaders? It is because of its proven benefits in improving memory and helping the brain deal better with stress. A Boston University study found that as little as three and a half hours of meditation training could change how the brain reacts to certain emotionally charged images.

Meditation also helps practitioners become aware of negative thoughts, and thus detach from them more easily. While even the Dalai Lama agrees that it's probably impossible to prevent negative thoughts and emotions from clouding our mind, meditation can help you let go of those thoughts. In fact, experienced meditators can let go of emotions and thoughts almost the instant they surface. They also develop better problem-solving abilities, higher levels of self-discipline, and an ability to bounce back from stress more easily.

Beyond inner peace, meditation has quantifiable benefits for the chronically stressed, as proven by a five-year Harvard Medical School study led by John Denninger. Denninger found that meditation produced the following benefits for his research subjects:

- improved sleep quality

- greater ease returning to a relaxed state after a moment of stress

- improved athletic performance due to greater ability to focus

- improved immune system

Regular meditation should be a part of every businessman's tool kit. And the best part is you need no special tools or training – you can start right now.

*Challenge yourself with the following 'How to' exercises:*

1) PLAN on meditating early morning and, if possible, near Nature. Mornings are a quiet time, and allow you better concentration.

2) FIND a quiet place to be your regular meditation spot, so your body recognizes this place for meditation and

responds accordingly. Avoid choosing the TV room or the kitchen because these may distract you. Find a quiet spot at your workplace as well to meditate.

3) SIT down in a position that's comfortable, but not so comfortable that you fall asleep.

4) BECOME watchful of your body. The easiest way to begin is by focusing on your breath.

5) DON'T fight your thoughts. Allow them to come, but don't cling to them. The small gaps between thoughts create the power in meditation.

6) WHENEVER you have a problem, take a few minutes to meditate. Sit quietly and look at the sky, ocean, or birds. After a few minutes, return to the problem. You'll be amazed at the renewed clarity that you'll bring to the issue.

7) YOUR actions during the day have an impact (positive or negative) on your meditation, so fill your day with good acts. When you serve others, it will have a positive impact on your meditation. As a parent/spouse, be loving, kind, caring and nurturing. As a business person, mentor people and help your customers.

# Chapter Six

# Striving for Harmony

*"Your hand opens and closes, opens and closes. If it were always a fist or always stretched open, you would be paralyzed. Your deepest presence is in every small contracting and expanding, the two as beautifully balanced and coordinated as birds' wings."*

– Rumi

The next two hours were spent in complete silence.

Richard furiously worked on the reports, carefully calculating and rechecking the figures. The team had done a good job with the estimates, but the overall picture was still not rosy enough to convince the channel partners to jump on the bandwagon yet, he told himself.

Finally, when he looked up after completing the report, he found Zoya sleeping.

He gazed at her for some time. There was a certain serenity even when she was sleeping, and yet a certain liveliness about her. It was like watching a mountain brook – calm yet bustling with life.

As if sensing, she opened her eyes and smiled.

"Are you done with your reports?' she asked, yawning and stretching her legs.

"Not yet. But I am getting close. Actually, I have a board meeting right after the conference. That's what's going to make or break us for the next few years. So I can't afford a slip-up," he replied.

"Still a lot of window dressing to be done, I gather?" she asked, grinning.

"I hate to admit it but you're right. How did you guess?"

"Well I didn't just fall down from the sky like Mary Poppins and pick up the paintbrush. I have done my time on your side of the planet. So I have an idea of what it entails," she replied.

"Interesting! Where were you working on?" Richard asked.

"After I completed my Masters in Fine Arts, I worked with an interior design company for about two years. Then I joined an architectural and interior design firm for the next three years, before finally taking the plunge on my own," she replied, adding, "But what about you? You started with a business and then took a job. Usually people do it the other way around."

"Well, in my case, I wanted to be on my own. So business was the first choice. I started my workshop while I was still studying," he replied.

"Yes, you mentioned that. So what was this urge to be on your own so soon?" she asked.

"I kind of figured that financial success pretty much defined everything about you – your status in life, your circle of friends, the opportunities you could explore. And I wanted to make sure I was always ahead of the game."

"Was your dad running a business as well?"

"No. He worked as a foreman in a construction company. He joined as a worker and retired as a foreman. Not exactly a big jump on his career scale," he said with a shrug.

"Maybe he never wanted to?" she countered.

"I think he wanted a lot of things but didn't really have the guts to get it. Most of the time he would be away from home. The rest of the time he spent in either creating a ruckus or giving us the silent treatment. It was as if we were responsible for his misery."

"Wow, you seem to have a lot of unexpressed rage against your father," Zoya said.

"I guess, I do," he said matter-of-factly. "So, after my mother died, I finally found an excuse to leave home," he added in a quiet voice.

"How did she die?"

"She had liver cancer. We found out very late. She was gone in three months. But I think her decline had started much earlier," he said.

"And your siblings?"

"I have an older brother and a younger sister. My brother runs a small construction firm in Houston, and my sister is an elementary school teacher. She lives with her family in San Antonio."

"And your dad?"

"He is in a retirement home in San Antonio. I haven't seen him for 16 years. My sister checks on him occasionally."

"Okay."

"I have a son, William. He is eight now. He lives with my ex-wife in LA. She is a professor of Physics at UCLA."

"That's nice. So how often do you get to see him?" she asked.

"Well, I do try to catch up with him once every two months. But my work schedule is such that I always have to be on the move. Plus, meeting him means upsetting his schedule. It's best he gets a stable home environment. "

"Maybe you should let him decide," she said.

"He's too young to decide. And I don't ever want him to suffer the way I did."

"So you think you suffered because you had an unstable home environment?"

"Of course! That and well…" he replied, letting his sentence linger midway.

"Well?"

"Well, I think we should get back to you."

"Hmm," she said, nodding.

"Hmm?"

"I mean, I guess you are right. Stability trumps love any day." she said softly as she smiled.

# Bringing It to Life: Messages from Chapter Six – Striving for Harmony

## *The Storyline*

Richard is divorced, talks to his son only once every few months and hasn't talked to his father for 16 years. There is little, if any, harmony between his business and personal lives.

## *Messages*

*"I believe that being successful means having a balance of success stories across the many areas of your life. You can't truly be considered successful in your business life if your home life is in shambles."*

– Zig Ziglar

## *Reflect on the following questions:*

- Are you clear what work-life balance means to you?

- Do you spend time with people who are important to you?

- Do you regularly prepare a 'not to do' list against a never-ending 'to do' list?

- Do you regularly practice the Hour of Power: 20 minutes of exercise, 20 minutes of reading, and 20 minutes of meditation each morning?

- Do you focus on the 20 percent of things that give you 80 percent of results and benefits in each area?

- Do you schedule your most important activities first thing in the morning?

- Do you know where you spent your 168 hours last week?

- Do you emphasize results or activities?

- Do you write down your goals every morning?

Contrary to what we may think, striking a work-life balance doesn't make us less effective. In fact, it only makes us better workers than those who burn themselves out by focusing on work at the cost of family, health and harmony.

Many senior executives complain that they have too many demands, too many interruptions and distractions. They struggle to prioritize and end up firefighting despite their best efforts. For them, work-life balance is an aspiration, albeit an elusive one. They often feel that if they eke out time for their family and personal needs, they will fall behind in their careers.

The truth is that a balanced approach to work and life leads to more success. By creating synergy between the body, mind and the soul you will be far more energetic and productive than someone who leads an imbalanced life.

All of us are blessed with the same 168 hours in a week. However, while a few achieve breakthroughs in life, the majority merely trudge along, wondering why they can never find time to do the things they want to.

The ability to concentrate and use your time well is important if you want to succeed in business or in other areas of your life, and a well-balanced life is the best tool for that. When you are spiritually, mentally, physically, socially and economically balanced, then you're a success.

The key is to look after your business, your balance (work, health, social circle and family) and your beyond (spirituality, giving, purpose); and not prioritize one over the other. Paying equal attention to all three aspects will strengthen you as a person.

It is not just that harmony benefits your life – lack of harmony hurts it, in real tangible ways. The World Health Organization estimates that stress costs American businesses $300 billion a year. The *2012 Workplace Survey* released by the *American Psychological Association* suggests that many Americans report chronic work-related stress. Around 41 percent said they "feel tense or stressed out during the workday," an uptick from the previous year's 36 percent. In its annual wellness report, Employee Assistance Program provider ComPsych found that 38 percent of employees can't stop thinking about emotional, health, financial and job concerns.

Work-life balance not only results in happiness and personal success, it can even lead to business innovation. Richard Branson, CEO of Virgin Airlines, has noted that some of his best ideas come when he engages his children in conversations about his work.

Melinda Gates sums it up well: "The only thing I care about on the day I die is that people think I was a great mom, family member, and friend."

*Challenge yourself with the following 'How to' exercises:*

1) MAKE balance a personal priority and be clear what balance means to you.

   Do what Dr. Stephen Covey would call 'first things first': making sure that business, balance and beyond all play their parts.

2) SPEND time with loved ones; and also set aside time to improve your health and do things that matter to you, like pursuing a hobby. If you don't spend quality time with your loved ones or do things that are important in your life, someone or something less important will take up your time.

3) PREPARE a 'not to do' list, not a 'to do' list. This will remove non-essentials from your life. How do you make a 'not to do' list? List everything that must be done in your life; delegate as much as you can; next, eliminate what is not necessary, then prioritize and execute what is left.

4) PRACTICE the Hour of Power: 20 minutes of exercise, 20 minutes of reading and 20 minutes of meditation each morning.

5) OBSERVE the Power of the Hour: schedule an appointment with yourself midday to regroup, reflect and reprioritize. This will make your afternoons more productive.

6) RECORD where your time goes. When you do this, you become more aware and alert, thereby improving your focus and allocation of time.

7)  REMEMBER THAT SLOW is fast – when you slow down time spent with your family, you notice a lot more about them, and have time to actually hear them out. Consequently, your relationships get better as your attention and care create impact. Or, for example, if you start eating slowly, you can enjoy your food better and feel full faster.

8)  FOCUS on the 20 percent of things that give you 80 percent of value.

9)  WRITE the top three goals you want to accomplish the next day before you go to bed, and work on them exclusively (at least till 2 pm the next day). Then you can take care of smaller tasks.

10)  SPEND quality time with business partners, colleagues, customers, spouse, partner, children and parents.

11)  DEFINE what a successful day and week means to you. Then set about achieving the same.

12)  ACCOUNT for your time, prioritize quality time and align time spent with your purpose; only then will you start managing time, instead of having time manage you!

# Chapter Seven

# Finding Meaning in Tragedy

*"The wound is the place where the Light enters you."*

– Rumi

"And you? What's the deal with you?" Richard asked. They had just finished lunch and Zoya was unwrapping a chocolate bar.

"Me? Well, I started out with a normal family. My parents, a younger brother and myself. We were your typical Indian family. My dad is an architect and my mom is a homemaker. And when I say a homemaker, I mean a homemaker. You see, my mom is one of those people who take their jobs very seriously – from embroidering her own tablecloths, making jams and preserves, inviting people for those elaborate five-course dinners – the whole caboodle."

"So were you always like this?"

"You mean a little cuckoo?" she asked, mock serious.

"No! Not at all! Please don't get me wrong. I meant..." he said, shifting uncomfortably in his seat.

"I understand, Mr. Wiseman. Just wanted to see you squirm a little," she grinned. "Well, I was a little too stubborn as a child. And yes, I had a lot of questions. I had to know the 'why' of things. Otherwise it was very difficult to persuade me to do anything. But I think the turning point was the death of my little brother. He was only four. And his death shook me apart."

"What happened?"

"It was an accident. A freak accident and I think that's what made it so much more painful," she murmured. "I remember the day distinctly. It's so alive in my memory as if it happened just yesterday."

Zoya continued, "It was late June and it had been raining since morning. So we were sent home early from school.

My mom had an inflamed wisdom tooth and was away for a dental appointment. Our house help, Vimla, had been instructed to put us to bed after lunch. But Kabir had been throwing tantrums since that morning to be allowed to go out and float his paper boat. He had learnt to make them in his crafts class. So, once the maid left our room, he slipped out into the garden. We lived in an old rambling bungalow in Pune then. It had a large overgrown garden and a long cobbled driveway.

"I think it was still drizzling when he stepped out. He sat under a large neem tree near the boundary wall and waited for the rain to stop. We later found his jacket under the tree. That same day, my dad had to rush back home in the afternoon to collect some drawings. He drove in, parked the car in the driveway and went in to get them. We had a white Ambassador, which had been a part of our family for as long as I can remember. Anyway, he was back within minutes and got in the car. The glass was foggy with the rain and when my dad backed the car, there was a dull thud. At first he thought that he had backed into the parapet on the side. But when he got out and looked, it was all over. My brother was gone.

"Somehow, in those few minutes, my brother had slipped behind the car to float his boat in the drainage gully that separated the garden from the driveway.

"I heard our maid scream, and woke up with a start. When I rushed to the window, I saw my dad holding the limp body of my brother in his arms and looking dazed and Vimla, standing nearby and wailing. I don't remember much of the day after that.

"But our lives changed. It was as if our whole life was suddenly submerged in guilt. My mother felt responsible because she had left us alone with the help. I did too, because I was the older sister and was supposed to look out for Kabir. I had known that my brother had quietly slipped out of the room, but had been too sleepy to go after him."

"And your dad?" asked Richard softly.

"And yes, my dad. He was so utterly shattered by grief and remorse, that he simply stopped coming home in the evenings. It was as if he was afraid of being near us, of hurting us. After that, I saw him only on weekends or late at night, his bent frame quietly poring over his blueprints in the study.

"At first, my mom tried to rally us back together, but Dad seemed unable or unwilling to get over his guilt.

"I grew up with this memory coloring my every experience. I think at first I couldn't comprehend the loss. One day my brother was there – his feisty, boisterous, lanky, three-foot frame fighting with me for the first raw mango off our tree; and the next moment, he had simply vanished from my life. For a long time, I used to feel guilty for enjoying a cupcake or drinking hot chocolate without him. His memory followed me everywhere.

"As I grew up, I began to read a lot and experiment with philosophies and religions, desperately trying to seek answers. I was 17 I think, when I attended a meditation program that involved Sufi whirling.

"That day I had skipped classes to attend the session. Until then, I had no idea as to what it entailed, so had no expectations either. In the beginning, the whirling was a little nauseating, but I kept on, determined to complete the whole set of movements.

"And then the tempo of the music began to rise and I kept on whirling faster and faster. It was as if the movement had acquired a life of its own and I was simply floating along like a dead leaf. Suddenly, there came a moment where I felt as if I had stopped and was watching my body continue to whirl around me. It was a surreal feeling. I can't really put it in words. I felt calm, detached and strangely peaceful. For the first time in many years, I could finally stand apart from my grief. And though I couldn't articulate it then, I knew at that moment that my grief was not me. I could see how my parents and I had allowed grief and guilt to consume our lives instead of using it to bring us closer as a family. My brother had lost his life when he was 4, but we had lost the following 12 years to numbing guilt. Instead of celebrating his memory or celebrating each other's presence, we had each chosen to smother our lives with darkness and despair."

Zoya continued, "That day, when I came out of the session, the sun was just beginning to set. The sky was a rich hue of orange, pink and red with a smattering of purple flecks. A bunch of sparrows was creating a ruckus in the nearby pawpaw tree. A hawker was selling bright pink cotton candy. I bought one and as its soft wool melted in my mouth, I felt my senses come alive for the first time in many years. I could see, smell, hear and taste everything so vividly, so intensely.

"Since then, I decided that I will not stop feeling miserable. I have already lost so much time. Now I am determined to not miss anything, and want to experience everything in glorious technicolor. Nothing is good or bad anymore. Everything is an excuse to plunge into life even more passionately. Each moment is bursting with new experiences and stories. So I try not to attach myself to the past too much now. Because whenever I dwell on the past, I lose the present – this *now*, this alive, pulsating, and juicy NOW," she exclaimed animatedly.

"That's a wonderful approach to living. Most people would not be able to take it that way," Richard remarked with quiet wonder.

"Hmm, I don't know. When you spend a major part of your childhood trying to play numb, your spirit is bound to revolt and break out one day. You just need an outlet. For me it was through that dance," she answered.

"Yes, but it's not easy to deal with the loss of a loved one," he said, thinking about his past.

"I think it's because we view death negatively. But we forget that life and death are simply two polarities of human experience. Because of our fear of letting go, we create a division between them. Yet the undeniable fact remains that both life and death are entwined at the core. We start dying the moment we are born," she replied, passing him a piece of chocolate.

"But in spite of its inevitability, we are unable to accept it. We find it difficult to deal with a loss of any kind, for that matter," he replied, accepting the chocolate.

"Yes, I find it hard to believe that people become inconsolable even at the prospect of losing a job," she added.

"That's because our job, our work is much more than just a means of livelihood; it defines us," Richard said, a tad defensively.

"Yes, but you are not simply your job. There is so much more to you. In fact, I find it so funny that when you ask people to introduce themselves they always describe their occupation. Only when you probe further do other details start emerging," Zoya said.

"Well, come to think of it, if we lose a job, we lose our sense of identity. That's one of the reasons many people get very disillusioned when they retire. They seem to lose their sense of purpose. Suddenly, there is nothing to do, no place to be, no one to need you or value you," he explained.

"But we still have ourselves! And every ending carries the possibility of a new beginning. So in effect, death is not the end but simply another opportunity to resurrect, to let go of all that no longer serves us," she said.

"You're right, but you see everything we deem important seems to arise from our past, including our beliefs, opinions, relationships; everything that is familiar and comfortable around us. This is why our attachment to the past is very strong and we don't want to give it up, even if it has stopped serving us or has become a source of pain... because it is the only thing we know," he replied.

"That reminds me of an old Sufi story by Osho. There was a poor woodcutter who was fed up with his miseries. Every day during prayer, he would question God: 'Why me? Everybody seems to be so happy. Why am I the only one suffering?' One day, out of great desperation, he prayed to

God, 'You can give me anybody else's suffering and I am ready to accept it. But take mine; I cannot bear it anymore.'

"That night, he had a beautiful dream. God appeared in the sky and said to everybody, 'Bring all your sufferings into the temple.' Everybody was tired of their own suffering – in fact everybody, at one time or another, was envious of his neighbor. Each felt that he had been given a larger burden, something that he did not deserve. So, people gathered their sufferings in bags and reached the temple. They were ecstatic. Finally their prayers had been heard. Our man also rushed to the temple.

"God asked everyone to put their bags of suffering by the temple walls. Then He declared: 'Now you can choose. Anybody can take any bag.'

"Surprisingly, the woodcutter rushed towards his own bag before anybody else could take it! But he was in for a shock, because everybody else also rushed to their own bags, and happily chose it again. What was the matter? For the first time, everybody had seen others' miseries – their bags were as big, or even bigger! And everybody returned home happy that day. Our fear of the unknown is so high that we don't mind clinging to our misery," Zoya concluded.

"So true," Richard exclaimed.

"At least your bag is familiar. To choose somebody else's bag... who knows what kind of sufferings it will contain!" she added.

"Yes, you're right," he replied, laughing.

"Rumi says: 'die before you die'. It means live each moment fully. Then, when the moment dies, there is no pain or regret because you'd already lived it completely," said Zoya.

"Come to think of it, it makes sense in business as well. If we stop fearing change, then each moment in business can move beyond our ego to an opportunity for transformation," Richard said.

"You're right," replied Zoya, but as she stretched back in her seat, her attention was drawn to the window. "Oh my God! Did you see that?" she suddenly exclaimed.

# Bringing It to Life: Messages from Chapter Seven – Finding Meaning in Tragedy

### The Storyline

Zoya lost her brother in a tragic accident when he was four years old. Her family was overcome with guilt and became disconnected from each other. But Zoya was able to use this tragedy to eventually discover meaning and truth in her own life.

### Messages

*"Grief can be the garden of compassion. If you keep your heart open through everything, your pain can become your greatest ally in your life's search for love and wisdom."*

– Rumi

### Reflect on the following questions:

- Do you believe that there is some meaning in every loss?

- Do you forgive others?

- Do you forgive yourself?

- Are you waiting to be happy one day??

- Are you carrying the baggage of the past and future?

- Do you believe in the saying: 'destiny is in the journey'?

- Do you carry self-inflicted guilt?

- Are you able to turn a minus into a plus?

- The time to live is now; if we are not happy in this moment, when will we ever be happy?

Regardless of the situation, we can always choose how to respond. Every sadness or seemingly untoward situation carries the seed of learning and opportunity.

Everything given in this life is given in trust by the Divine, as a gift. When it is gone, it is a good memory to be grateful for. It was never really yours.

Nelson Mandela was imprisoned for 27 years for opposing Apartheid. After his release, he said: "I am working now with the same people who threw me into jail, persecuted my wife, hounded my children from one school to the other… and I am one of those who is saying: Let us forget the past, and think of the present." He was able to transform South Africa through authenticity, commitment and consistency of message. One of Mandela's greatest legacies is starting the national healing process from the moment he was released.

Viktor Frankl survived a Nazi concentration camp and wrote a book, *Man's Search for Meaning*, about the importance of having  purpose in life. Frankl noticed that his fellow prisoners typically lost their sense of purpose before they sickened and died. This taught him that a sense of purpose can help us through the most difficult of circumstances.

You may be wondering how this lesson applies to business. On September 11, 2001, airlines were forced to shut down for days while the United States of America was recovering from the unprecedented terrorist attacks. This meant that all airline passengers, flight attendants and pilots were stranded across the country. Instead of merely sitting and waiting, Southwest Airlines encouraged employees to take passengers bowling or to the movies to pass the time.

Following 9/11, the airline industry had been badly affected, and many airlines were forced to cut their workforce by up to 20 percent. Instead of following the trend, Southwest Airlines announced only three days after 9/11 that the airline would keep all its employees and start a $179.8 million profit-sharing program for them.

Southwest CEO James Parker believed that because Southwest had built its company on sound business principles for the past 30 years, they were able to handle the crisis better than other airlines.

Businesses can find inspiration in smaller setbacks. Starbucks' founder Howard Schultz was inspired by his father's struggles with poor health to make Starbucks the first American company to give health care options to part-time employees. Schultz used his life experiences, including the tragedy and pain of his father's struggles, to build a company that was a reflection of his personal values.

Tragedy struck the company in 1997 when three employees were killed in a bungled robbery at one of its Washington D.C. outlets. Instead of issuing a press release or calling legal counsel, Schultz flew straight to D.C. to comfort a hurting store and community. He spent the entire week with the employees and their families. Schultz's compassion and incredible leadership helped heal those closest to the tragedy.

Toyota belatedly recalled 2.3 million vehicles because of faulty brakes in October 2014. Many complaints and lawsuits were filed. It appeared as if the Toyota brand would be tarnished for years to come. Instead of only issuing press statements and giving interviews, Toyota quickly responded by offering a live conversation on one of the most popular communities on the web: Digg (despite the community behind Digg generally being quite hostile to corporations).

While the fallout from the recalls was massive, Toyota's openness greatly helped to minimize damage to the company's reputation. Toyota's decision to face the misfortune allowed customers to maintain their confidence in the company.

Many Texas banks were failing in the late 1980s, and TDIndustries was hurt greatly by lack of funds. The company leadership informed employees that instead of filing for bankruptcy, they were going to pay out the Defined Retirement Plan to its employees, and asked employees to use that money to reinvest in the company.

Because of the company's transparency and trust in their employees, they responded by investing 30 percent more than the company asked for. The money helped stabilize the company and it weathered the rough financial spell. TDIndustries has consistently been on Forbes' Best Companies to Work for list.

Knowing how to find sense and meaning in tragedy is an important skill for any businessman. Think how you reacted to your own past tragedies, and how some of your friends, family or colleagues reacted to theirs. You will notice positive and negative responses. Learn from them – notice which ones were helpful, and which ones caused sadness or stress – and adapt them to your situation, should the need arise.

Lebanese poet Khalil Gibran says: "Your pain is the breaking of the shell that encloses your understanding. Even as the stone of the fruit must break, that its heart may stand in the sun, so must you know pain; and could you keep your heart in wonder at the daily miracles of your life, your pain would not seem less wondrous than your joy."

### Challenge yourself with the following 'How to' exercises:

1) THIS too shall pass. Whatever is happening now is temporary. Ask yourself: How is this problem going to impact me 10, 20 or 50 years from now? This approach works for both business and personal tragedies.

2) RESPOND as positively as possible to tragedy. In any situation, it's your choice to be positive or negative. There is a saying: "Two men looked out through prison bars. One saw the mud; the other saw the stars." Both were in the same situation but each reacted differently to it. It may be hard to be positive, but it will help you process the tragedy more quickly, and learn lessons from it, too.

3) ASK how tragedy offers opportunity. Sometimes from breakdowns, come breakthroughs!

4) CREATE meaning from loss. If you have lost someone, ask how you can honor them by helping others.

5) EVERYTHING given in this life is given as a gift. When it's gone, it's a good memory to be grateful for. It was never really yours.

6) ASK yourself how crying, feeling guilty or feeling depressed will help you overcome the problem. It's important to process your feelings, but dwelling on them is counterproductive.

7) EVERYTHING happens for the highest good even though it may not appear to be so at the moment. Even prophets and saints underwent suffering and tragedy. Ask yourself: what can I do to turn my business tragedy into an opportunity? If you got fired from a job, you now have an opportunity to study, pursue your dream job, or travel for a few months. So either you take one of these opportunities or wallow in self-pity. The former advances you, the latter is destructive.

8) WHEN something negative happens, understand that you have been endowed with the capacity to overcome it.

# Chapter Eight

# Unleashing Your Power Within

*"Nothing can dim the light which shines from within."*

– Maya Angelou

Zoya was looking out of the little airplane window and pointing at the clouds. She looked as happy as a child, her curls framing her eager face.

She caught Richard looking at her and exclaimed, "Oh, don't you simply love this? It's like we have walked into a buffet of cotton candy!"

Richard smiled at her and said, "You seem to love everything, don't you? The trees, the clouds, the little packets of airline peanuts."

She looked at him for a while before asking, "What's there not to love? Isn't loving the center of our existence?"

"Is it?" he asked.

"I think it is. Can you think of any other feeling which can single-handedly pull us, cajole us, stretch us, thresh, shake, mold us and force us to become bigger than we think we are?" she asked, that familiar incandescence lighting up her eyes again.

"So is love the central ideology of Sufism?" Richard asked, closing his laptop and giving her his full attention.

"Sufism is not concerned with ideologies or beliefs. But yes, in its very essence, Sufism is about love, intense, all-consuming love with the Divine. For Sufism, the whole of creation is a manifestation of the Divine. Even airline peanuts," she said with a chuckle.

"The Sufis call their vision *Tassawuri,* a loving prayer of existence. And so our practice is about falling in love with the Divine, submerging in it, becoming one with it," she added. "In fact, if stripped down to their bare minimum, all religions are essentially about love," she explained.

"So it's fundamentally a love affair with the Divine?" he asked.

"Yes. You can say that. But on a lighter note, it means simply growing in awareness. Once you start becoming aware of how interconnected everything is, it becomes very difficult to do anything against your spirit. Because now you know that what you do to others you do to yourself. The feeling of separation disappears. Then your whole being becomes an outpouring of love.

"In fact, don't you think love is the starting point of everything in life?" Zoya asked.

"I guess so. Even at work, it's important to love what you do. However, for so many of us, it's just a means of livelihood. It's a pity we have such a cursory attitude towards a job or business, which consumes almost 75 percent of our waking time," he added.

"Well, you can call it conditioning. Most of us as children are led to believe that work and play are two separate affairs. As a result, we grow up equating work to boring and play to fun," she said.

"True. I must say though, even as a child, my passion was machines. When I was around ten, I had dismantled our dishwasher to find out if we could design an automatic bath," Richard said with a mischievous grin.

"Are you serious?" she asked, raising her eyebrows in amazement.

"Yes, I hated taking baths as a kid; too much work every morning. And the dishwasher seemed like a clever device. Luckily, I had teachers who encouraged my passion and guided me in the right direction," he answered contentedly.

"But my point is that we often ignore the deeper significance of things we enjoy. We usually think that they are an impractical means of making a living and that work necessarily has to be boring or unemotional to be deemed worthwhile," he explained, his whole being now animated.

In the few hours since she had met him, Zoya had not seen Richard so impassioned. She could not suppress a smile. He became a little confused when he saw her smiling but got back to his point.

"Children are often lured into professions by the promise of a good life. But we don't understand that the good life follows what you love doing and not the other way around. It's not surprising that children end up doing something chosen for them by their parents and society and not their passion," he concluded, taking a sip of water.

"Hmm. For me it was colors. When I was four, my parents were shocked to find me happily coloring the living room walls with some unused paint, while the babysitter slept peacefully nearby," she reminisced, her eyes twinkling with amusement.

"What did they do?" he asked laughing.

"My mom was livid. Along with the walls, I had managed to splash ample paint on her expensive paisley upholstered sofa. But my dad seemed amused, though he tried to keep a straight face when my mom glowered at him," she said, trying to suppress a giggle.

"But later, when I was seriously considering master's degree in art while at college, they both were quite skeptical.

Dad wanted me to stick to architecture or engineering, while mom was trying to get me married. That was their way of securing my future. I snuck out of my room to take the entrance exam. Luckily, I cleared the tests, both for engineering and art school. Finally, dad relented. But not all my friends were so lucky. You can't just blame their parents. Most of my classmates didn't even know what they really wanted to do," she said.

"But it's sad to live life without doing what you love. I think every person is born unique. Everyone has their own special gift. But most of us are never able to know or use this gift," Richard responded.

"This is because to find your gift you have to look deep within yourself. And not everyone is lucky enough to know his or her special talent in school. For some, the discovery might happen much later. So, what would you advise people who are still trying to find their calling?" she asked, propping her head on her arm.

"Hmm, let's see. You must ask yourself three things. First, what makes you come alive? Something that you not only enjoy but also admire."

"Something you admire?" she asked, suddenly curious.

"We are all taken in by different ideas at different times. And a lot of us spend considerable time flirting with lofty concepts which we misconstrue as our passion. So the key here is to pay attention to those ideas that compel us to look further, to experiment, to put our best foot forward, and make us go, 'WOW!'"

"Agree with you there," she said.

"Second, what kind of life do I want to create for myself? If you are looking for a career in acting, then wanting to live in the country might not be a bright idea in the beginning. Different careers demand different lifestyles. You have to be ready to change yours if needed.

"Third, what kind of skills can I bring to my chosen path?" he said, inquiringly.

"Ahem, I see the CEO surfacing," Zoya answered in mock military voice.

He laughed.

"But seriously. For instance, in your profession, liking art and becoming an artist are two different things. You might have a good eye for art but it doesn't necessarily mean that you will be good at painting. So it's best to be honest about the aptitude and skills you bring to the table. And even if you have the required skills, a lot of work is needed to hone them, before you can actually start creating good work.

"Let's look at it this way. Somebody might want to be a singer. But if asked if he would like to be able to sing like Michael Jackson, he might answer: 'Oh he was too talented. I could never do that.' That's another way of saying I am not committed enough to try," Richard said.

"Yeah, the ways of the ego are subtle. We think we are being practical, but practicality is often a clever ruse for hiding a lot of our inadequacies," she added.

"Or another popular method is being armchair commentators, criticizing those who do try."

"Yes. The easiest thing in life is being a spectator," Zoya commented, offering Richard the peanuts.

He munched thoughtfully, then said, "But I guess at times you can't help it. Not all of us find the opportunity. Some have to give up their dreams midway."

"The woods would be quiet if no bird sang but the one that sang best. The joy is in the singing. When I paint, I paint because I enjoy painting. Of course, I am motivated by the monetary aspects. But they don't guide my hand. I do it because there is nothing else I would rather be doing," she added.

"So are you saying that it's wrong to aspire to have a goal, or be the best?" he countered.

"If you limit yourself to being the best among others, then yes. Because in that very aspiration, you have paved the way to invite misery. Because life is too vast to be confined to your definition of the best. There will always be someone who is going to be better than you or your work. The only aspiration that matters is choosing to be *your* best. Only then can your being, your craft actually flower," she concluded.

"Hmm, you're right. When I topped high school, I was on top of the world. But when I came to undergraduate school on a scholarship, the first year was a big eye-opener. Suddenly, I was not the best, just one among all the rest of the best," he remarked.

"Exactly my point. I feel we have done a lot of damage to children by frightening them with the prospect of being a failure. If only we could view life as an adventure, an opportunity to learn, and not as a series of successes and failures, we could be so much more creative and courageous. For example, coming back to you, it was not all a smooth ride to the top. You must have encountered a lot of challenges. But your passion for engineering sustained you. In fact I am sure, product design must be one of the unique selling propositions of your company today," she added.

"You are right, it is. But to be honest, the last few years have not been all that noteworthy," he replied.

"So maybe you need to take a break to revive your creative spark?" Zoya suggested.

"Well, I don't look after the R&D function any more. Strategy and operations consume most of my time. But we have a good young team. The gap right now is finding a capable person to lead the team. And with low margins and tough competition we haven't been able to find the right person."

"So why don't you step in?"

"Me? It's not that simple," he said, giving her an incredulous look.

"Why not?" she asked.

"For one, my current role hardly leaves me any time to get into the details. Second, going back to my previous role might mean a step down from my current position. It might not bode well for my career in the long run."

"But you have already been the CEO. You reached your goal. You proved yourself to yourself," she exclaimed. "Unless of course engineering no longer excites you."

"Oh, no! That's my first love," he ventured quickly.

"So, there might be another reason. Are you now attached to your position and the perks it offers you?" she asked softly.

"Well, if I am, I don't think there is anything wrong with

that. I have a certain place, a position in life because I worked hard for it!" he firmly added.

"There's nothing wrong with that as long as you enjoy it. But we should remember that whatever we own also starts owning us. And soon, you have to ask whether *you are* running the show or *the show* is running you," she answered slowly and then looked up at him.

He stared back but didn't say anything.

"Anyway, I think I might be overstepping my limits here. After all, I have no idea how your business works. And yes, we do operate in a cut-throat society where a momentary sidestep might cost you a lot. But then again, what are you so scared of losing?" she asked, still looking at him.

He smiled and kept silent.

But when she too didn't speak, he picked up the gauntlet.

"Hmm, so I guess this entire journey of love begins with teaching children to do what they love," he ventured.

"No. Every journey of love begins with self-love. Parents must first and foremost help children to love themselves," she responded.

"Hmm, self-love. Aren't you venturing into some good old narcissism here? Don't you think we have enough selfish people already? I mean after our entire conversation about love and the need to share, don't you think we should spread love instead of hoarding it for ourselves?" he countered.

"There is a difference between self-love and being selfish. Self-love becomes selfish only if it never moves beyond its own self. Plus how can you give something that you don't already have?" she asked.

"What do you mean?"

"I'll tell you an anecdote from the life of Rabiya, a famous Sufi mystic. Then we'll discuss what I mean.

"One evening, people saw Rabiya searching for something on the street in front of her hut. They gathered around and asked her, 'What is the matter? What are you searching for?' Rabiya replied, 'I have lost my needle.' So they offered to help her and started looking around. Finally, after searching for a while, when they still couldn't find the needle, someone asked, 'Rabiya, the street is big and the night is just descending and soon there will be no light. The needle is such a small thing – unless you tell us exactly where it has fallen, it will be difficult to find it.'

"Rabiya answered, 'The needle has fallen inside my house.'

"They said, 'Have you gone mad? If the needle has fallen inside the house, why are you searching here?' Rabiya responded, 'Because the light is here. Inside the house there is no light.'

"They were flummoxed by her reply. Then someone said: 'Even if the light is here, how can we find the needle if it has not been lost here? The right way would be to bring light inside the house so that you can find the needle.'

"Rabiya laughed, 'You are such clever people about small things. When are you going to use your intelligence to seek your inner life? I have seen you all searching outside, and I know from my own experience that what you are searching for is lost within. Your logic is that because your eyes can see what's outside and because the light is outside, what you are searching for is also outside.'

"So it is pointless to search for bliss outside when it lies within us. Similarly, it's no use searching outside for love when you can't even love yourself. In fact, self-love is the source of all love. It is the starting point for trusting one's own self. And once you begin to trust yourself, you can then begin to trust others. Then there is no need to give in to other people's opinions about you just to feel accepted or loved. Because you already feel that way. You can then be more authentic. And you can share your love, unconditionally," Zoya explained with a smile.

He smiled and shook his head. She gave the weirdest of examples to make you question life.

"Hmm, may be you're right. But love is still a risky proposition."

"Hmm. The ways of the ego are subtle," she said, suppressing a smile.

"What do you mean?"

"Sometimes to avoid rejection or disappointment, it's better to avoid love."

"So you think it is sour grapes in my case?"

"Oh no, I am not judging you. I am simply saying we like to cling to our own concepts of ourselves and our experiences. It's very difficult to let go; because letting go of your fears means letting go of your ego, and fear and ego are best friends. Each is strengthened by the other. In this context, I love how Rumi puts it. He says: 'Your task is not to seek love, but merely to seek and find all the barriers within yourself that you have built against it.'"

"Maybe you're right," he said, leaning on one side and nodding slowly.

"Or maybe I'm not," Zoya answered.

"But I agree, your self-love theory makes sense, even in business," he said.

"Really! How come?"

"Well it's often a challenge to create trust in teams. Competition often kicks in. So people end up working on their own and we're not able to leverage group synergy."

"So what do you do in such situations?"

"I think the fear of competition arises only when the individual is not sure about the value he brings to the table. And this happens when he hasn't spent time discovering and working on his strengths. Come to think of it, there is enough room for everybody to be their unique self," he said.

"To me, it's a lifelong process of self-discovery. And all those we meet are simply there to help us learn faster. We are continually merging and separating from one another. Any threatening person or situation is only a sign for us to look within. And sometimes we do need a shock to jolt us out of our complacency. Once you start accepting every experience and individual as a teacher, then there is no hate, only gratitude," she said.

"So if every journey of love begins with self-love, what is the end?" he asked.

"To become love. It's the only way to go beyond the duality of the self and experience the Divine. You become undivided and whole."

"Sounds beautiful. You have a way with words," he said.

"Thank you," she smiled, bowing her head in response.

"And on this poignant note, a small gift for you," Zoya said, taking out a package wrapped in handmade paper and handing it to Richard.

"You got me a gift! You didn't have to," he said, unwrapping the package.

"Well, gifts are never given because you need to. You give because you feel like sharing," she said with a quick shrug.

It turned out to be a small hardbound book.

"*The Essential Rumi?*" he exclaimed.

"It's a book of Rumi's poems."

"Thanks! When did you pick this up?" he asked, pleasantly surprised.

"Today, from the airport bookshop. Hope you enjoy it as much as I did," she said warmly.

"I'm sure I will."

# Bringing It to Life: Messages from Chapter Eight – Unleashing Your Power Within

### *The Storyline*

Zoya shares an anecdote with Richard from Sufi mystic Rabiya's life, which tells us that the answers we seek are often located within us, not outside.

### *Messages*

Oliver Wendell Holmes has said, "What lies before us and what lies behind us are tiny matters compared to what lies within us."

### *Reflect on the following questions:*

- Do you aim high enough?

- Have you got the right team?

- Do you believe that you can achieve your goals?

- Do you walk, talk, sleep and breathe like a winner irrespective of the situation?

- Have you overcome your ego and fear, which prevent you from unleashing your power within?

- Are you clear what success means to you?

- Do you take daily actions that are aligned with your goals?

Where is your real power? Is it in the title you carry? Is it in the possessions you have – a nice car, a big house, money in the bank? Is it in your status? No, your power is not outside you. It's within you. External power may feed your ego, but internal power is empowering; external power is temporary, internal power is permanent; external power is limited, internal power is limitless.

You have immense potential. You are endowed with enormous gifts. However, you are more than likely looking for this power outside, in the wrong places. When you take the journey within, you can tap into your true genius and discover the real beauty that lies there.

In the late twentieth century, renowned psychologist and philosopher William James famously observed that "the average person rarely achieves but a small portion of his or her potential."

Brian did not finish high school. Early in life, he did odd jobs and was even homeless for a while. One day, he asked himself: "Why is it that some people make more money and are more successful than others?" The answer was so simple. In his words, it knocked him into a different direction. He discovered that successful people wrote down their goals. So he did exactly that. And he started achieving those goals within 30 days. Soon, he moved from a boarding house to a small apartment and kept going from there. Over the years, he has taught millions how to tap into their power within.

NBA player Brandon Todd who stands 5'9" has been one of the shortest players in the history of basketball. He wanted to achieve the seemingly impossible goal of learning to dunk a basketball. Todd used an intense weight-training regimen, inspired by Russian weight lifters, to gain 85 pounds of muscle. He also engaged in running and jump training, and after three years of work, was finally able to achieve his goal. "I was willing to put myself through all this pain and anguish for that one moment to say: 'I can do it.'"

Rumi reminds us: "You are not a drop in the ocean. You are the entire ocean in the drop." Your eyes can see stars trillions of miles away. You may be small physically but you have enormous power inside you. Even the great physicists, Isaac Newton and Albert Einstein, were not able to use their full potential. No one can. If you were to live several lifetimes, you still would not exhaust the potential you have within.

One of the ways to unleash this power, as we've already discussed, is through meditation. Another way is to imagine what would you dare to attempt if you knew you could not fail? Each person is special and powerful. You have immense potential to tap your genius.

### Challenge yourself with the following 'How to' exercises:

1) BELIEVE you have this power: articulate your mission and purpose by writing them down. Ensure that your goals are aspiring and energizing. Read these statements every night before you go to sleep and every morning when you wake up; internalize them and evaluate weekly; and take small steps towards improvement every day.

2) Tap the gifts you are born with by asking yourself: "What comes naturally to me? What gives me energy?

What are my strengths? What work would I do if I won $40 million in a lottery?"

3) LOOK at past hurdles and events and see how you've been able to overcome them. Study the specific, unique ways that you solved your problems, and learn more about yourself from them.

4) REFRAME what power means: not the external trappings of achievement, but love, gratitude and the willingness to give.

5) Meditation will help you connect with the genius inside you, waiting to be discovered. Believe in your capacity for greatness and capitalize on your uniqueness.

6) MAKE THE FIVE COMMITMENTS. These come from Azim's book, *Business, Balance & Beyond*, and embody the word, POWER:

P: Power of Giving – the more you give, the more you have

O: Open the gifts you were born with – your Birthday Gifts – shine your light and inspire others to shine their light

W: Have a Winning Attitude – aim high to reach high

E: Enlightened Persistence – persist until you succeed, but exit if you're chasing the wrong goals

R: Rejuvenation – nourish your mind, your body and soul and be present so you can see the signs the Universe is giving you

# Chapter Nine

# Converting Corporate Politics into Creative Synergy

*"But that's the challenge – to change the system more than it changes you."*

– Michael Pollan

"So does Rumi influence a lot of your thinking?"

"Well, to be honest, there is something to learn from everybody. But yes, Rumi inspires me," Zoya replied.

"Hmm, all the more reason to read this book," Richard said slowly, with a smile.

"Rumi always leads from the heart. So whenever there is a tussle between what I want to do and what feels right, his words offer me a lot of insight," she added with a smile.

"So, do you end up doing what feels right versus what you want to do?" he asked in a teasing tone.

"Well they are not always contrary, you know!" she answered in mock anger.

"And other times?" he persisted.

She replied, "Well, most of the time I do what feels right. But I admit there are times when I give in to my ego. Sometimes the rationalizations are so good that it's easy to sidestep what's right. But eventually you do always realize if you haven't been true to yourself. There's that tiny niggling but persistent voice at the back of your head that is not very easy to ignore for long."

"But will it not be too late by then?" he asked.

"In India, we have a saying: 'The day begins the moment you open your eyes!' So even if it's late, it's never too late to stop the situation from worsening. After all, who are we to decide when it's too early or too late? The important thing is to do the right thing. The result is never in our hands. Only our action is. And that is our only responsibility."

"Hmm, you're right. Even though we lay a lot of emphasis

on setting goals in business, we are not always able to control the results. Goals are very important, but valuing the process of action and execution is equally important," he replied.

"Well, life and business are not independent of each other. Our life is a sum total of our work, our relationships, opinions, idiosyncrasies, everything... and how can the part be different from the whole?" she asked rhetorically.

"Great! And with that statement, you have made the entire concept of work-life balance redundant," he replied with a perceptible sigh.

"Oh, you are right! I guess I did," she laughed.

"So coming back to work, why did you leave your job?" he asked.

"I used to find the structured environment stifling. Plus office politics always exhausted me," she answered, wrinkling her nose.

"Hmm," he said, looking at her intently and nodding slowly, though not looking very convinced. "Can you elaborate?"

"Uhh...for example, there was this senior colleague I was working with at my first job. Though he was good, he had this penchant for putting everybody down. Crack sexist jokes, you know. Make sarcastic comments. A jerk of the highest order."

He laughed. "So what did you do?"

"I noticed that others usually avoided any confrontation with him. So in the beginning, I tried to ignore it. It was like school again, hoping you didn't cross paths with the class bully. But after a while, it started to get to me. I just couldn't keep quiet like the others. So I started talking back," Zoya replied.

"Wow, that must have really fired his engines," he said.

"Yeah, you are right. It was as if I had waved a red flag in front of him. And once he saw I wasn't backing down, he became even more aggressive. Every small situation became an opportunity for scoring brownie points. So, after a while, most of my work centered on thinking about the next smart retort or some plan to give it back to him."

"And your boss?"

"Well, he too was smart. He realized he had found a worthy stooge to do his bidding."

"So who won finally?"

"No one. I got a good break in another company. And then that bully colleague ceased to matter."

"And your other job?"

"Well, that was okay, too. But I like it much better on my own."

"So Mr. Jerk turned you off the corporate scene?" he asked, not willing to let go.

"Well in hindsight, I think I learnt a lot from him."

"Really? How is that?"

"Because of his shrewdness, I learnt to be sharper with my work. And, I am proud to say, after a while he even started to seem a little wary of me. I guess it was beginning to get tiring for him as well, this constant baiting."

"That's great! You seem to be doing well on your own now, without the added interference of us corporate sharks," Richard said, laughing.

"I guess." But she didn't look so sure now.

"So what's your normal day like, now that you are off the corporate bandwagon?"

"Well, I leave in the morning for my studio with my cat, Zorba. I have rented a studio apartment as my workspace. The apartment is small, but it's nice and airy, with a huge balcony. Plus it's adjacent to a park, so it's very green and quiet… perfect for me. I begin the day by working on pending assignments, or sometimes, I start on an altogether new canvas, whatever calls out to me that day; while Zorba patiently watches me from her purple rug near the window. After lunch at a nearby café and kitty treats for Zorba, I work till early evening. Then I pack my stuff, settle my paints and brushes for the night and go home. Later I spend the evening either meeting up with friends or catching up on my reading or experimenting with cooking.

"Every fortnight, I meet my gallery contacts and visit local exhibitions to get an overview of what's happening in the market. Luckily with the internet, it's easier to stay in touch with everything. Once a week, I teach art history at a liberal arts college. So all in all, a quiet and idyllic existence," she answered with a satisfied sigh.

"So what kind of art are you into? Watercolors?"

"I mostly paint in oil and acrylics. Would you like to see my work?"

"Oh yes! That would be great!"

She opened a folder on her phone and handed it to him.

There were a series of abstracts and landscapes with rich palettes. There were a few charcoals as well. But most of her work showed a clear preference for bold colors with broad, open brushstrokes. And though he found her style a tad too dramatic for his taste, it was difficult to ignore the raw unbridled energy and luminosity of her work. He was suddenly reminded of the expression, *gorgeously crazy*. He had overheard someone use this expression at a party. "She was good. In fact, she was quite good," he thought.

"This is good," he said.

"You like it, really?" she asked incredulously.

"Yes, I do! Why, you don't believe me?" he asked, raising an eyebrow.

"No, it's just that I thought it might be a little too dramatic for your taste," she replied.

"Oh, so you think I would naturally veer towards the dull, grey stuff?" he asked, sounding miffed and secretly wondering if his thoughts had been that transparent.

"No, not at all. I mean your style is probably a little understated," she explained hurriedly.

He laughed.

"Well, I agree my taste is a little more understated. But seriously I like your work. It has a strong vibe to it."

"Thanks."

"So, who are your clients?"

"Right now I sell my work to a couple of galleries and some of it gets sold through word of mouth. Recently, my work was featured in the *Women in Art 278* magazine," Zoya said.

"That's great. So what are your future plans?"

"I just want to spend the next few years experimenting

with new styles and media. Go beyond the easel. My dream is to perhaps get my work featured internationally."

"Okay. So what's stopping you?" asked Richard.

"Well, you need funds for one."

"And?"

"And success is not defined by your artistic ability alone. I would need to get a lot more aggressive about my work. There are a number of other factors involved. Like what kind of art is currently in demand. How marketable or viable the art is. How well you negotiate with the gallery or the client. Your contacts etc.," she added.

"So it involves a lot of networking as well?" he asked.

"Oh yes! It's a virtual jungle out there!"

"And you don't want to enter the jungle?" he added.

She laughed, but then continued on a serious note, "Yes. I like to concentrate on what I am good at."

"Hmm," he mumbled distractedly.

"Hmm?"

"Oh nothing!" he just waved his hand dismissively, but his face expressed something else.

She was about to ask what he meant, but held back. He seemed to be angling at something and she didn't want to give in just yet.

Just then the pilot announced the preparation for landing in Dubai.

The plane circled the Dubai airport for what seemed like a really long time and landed with a soft thud, rushing over the tarmac, straining against the momentum to finally settle down to a gentle stop on the landing strip.

After some time, the doors opened, and people stood up in a rush to get out. Most seemed to be looking forward to the unexpected stop in Dubai. They walked quickly towards the waiting shuttle, keen to avoid the harsh afternoon sun.

Everyone gave an appreciative sigh as they entered the cool, lavish Dubai airport. It was huge, opulent and resembled a high-end shopping mall with premium luxury brands vying for attention.

Since the stopover was three hours away, Richard and Zoya agreed to part ways and meet at a Starbucks café an hour before boarding.

Richard decided to finish his pending calls and Zoya decided to explore the sights and sounds.

## Bringing It to Life: Messages from Chapter Nine – Converting Corporate Politics to Creative Synergy

### *The Storyline*

Zoya withdrew from her corporate job because of office politics.

### *Messages*

*"Individual commitment to a group effort – that is what makes a team work, a company work, a society work, a civilization work."*

– Vince Lombardi

### *Reflect on the following questions:*

- Do you do what is right or what is easy?
- Do you strive for being real or fall into the political trap?
- Do you own up to your weaknesses and let others own up to theirs?
- Do you judge people even before you meet them?
- Do you say what you mean and mean what you say?
- Do you always keep your principles and purpose in sight?
- Do you feel the pressure to make your organization look good, no matter what?

- For politically dominant workplaces, this kind of influence is, of course, all too familiar. Backstabbing, gossiping and the dangerously flirtatious dance of the corporate moth around the office flame can be a pricey affair.

Man is an interdependent being. We all need each other's support to make a success of our personal endeavors. But we often mistake this interdependence for dependence and become accustomed to seeking people's approval or permission at the risk of betraying our own values and principles.

When NASA launched an internal investigation in the wake of the Challenger explosion, they made a startling discovery – many who worked on the project had misgivings about whether or not the shuttle was ready to be launched, but didn't speak up for fear that doing so would hamper their careers and make it seem like they did not have faith in the NASA program.

Can you relate to this pressure? Unfortunately, it can lead to poor performance and a poorer bottom line. A British survey found that office politics and gossip cost the UK 7.8 billion GBP in productivity loss each year, and that managers spend an hour a day dealing with such problems among their employees.

In the United States, the estimated productivity loss because of stress is more than $100 billion each year. While these statistics are alarming, most companies will not change the way they function until they truly understand the connection between politics and performance.

Even though it remains a problematic issue worldwide, there are steps you can take to fight it, such as open communication, encouraging constructive feedback and rewarding transparency.

*Challenge yourself with the following 'How to' exercises:*

1) DON'T play the politics game. Instead, focus on action, integrity and results.

2) WHEN a peer is gossiping or back-biting, walk away if you are unable to stop him from doing so; don't participate, otherwise you become an enabler.

3) TAKE CONTROL of corporate politics. If you're a leader, make it clear to your team that they'll be evaluated on performance and productivity, not politics.

4) ESTABLISH consequences for people who are political or negative, and reward those who focus on results and meritocracy.

5) NETWORK in positive ways; be a progressive influence and a good role model. Convey through your actions that you can be successful without engaging in politics, so others can follow in your footsteps.

# Chapter Ten

# Appreciating the Benefits
# of Receiving

*"You are important enough to ask and you are blessed enough to receive."*

– Wayne Dyer

Richard sauntered past the deli to reach the coffee shop. There were still ten minutes to their agreed meeting time, but he was done with his planned tasks for the day and strangely enough, couldn't wait to get back.

He immediately spotted the tall slender figure in blue. But Zoya was not alone. There were two other people with her. One was a slightly overweight man with a ponytail and a young woman dressed in a grey pencil skirt, who was shifting uncomfortably on her high heels.

He decided to wait and let them finish. Maybe they were people she knew from work or probably friends. It wouldn't be polite to intrude their conversation. He settled down on a nearby sofa next to the newspaper stand and picked one up, idly glancing at the news.

But his attention kept straying back to the trio. They were standing about 50 feet away. The man was standing with his feet slightly apart and seemed to be explaining something with gusto, which was also apparently a source of amusement to him because he would frequently lean forward to make a point, gesturing animatedly, and then throw his head back to laugh. The young woman next to him seemed to be lapping up his words and was regularly nodding in response.

But then he saw that something was off; it was obvious even from a distance. Zoya was not her usual ebullient self.

Though she was smiling and nodding her head, her body language seemed a little restrained, even guarded. Occasionally, she glanced around the hall as if looking for something, but would half-heartedly come back to the conversation. .

He decided to interrupt. When he was around ten feet away, she turned suddenly and saw him. He was happy to notice that she visibly brightened on seeing him.

"Hi!" Richard strolled forward, smiling towards the trio. The man next to her, who was still engaged in his monologue, seemed a little taken aback by the intrusion, but recovered quickly to smile back at him. Zoya immediately seized the gap to make the introductions.

"Richard, this is Mr. Bhushan Oberoi. He is–," she said.

"You can call me Bobby, sir," the man interrupted Zoya, leaning forward with a solemn bow. He extended his business card at a leisurely pace, deliberately flashing his Rolex in the process. Bobby was in his early forties. About five feet nine, he had fair skin and delicate features, which would have been called handsome at one time but had now softened and sagged a little, giving him a rather petulant childlike look. He was dressed in a natty beige linen suit with a light blue striped shirt and dark brown loafers.

"Bobby is the account director at The Blu Tulip. It's an interior design firm in Mumbai," Zoya said.

"Eh, actually, I am now the regional head, Zoya. And we have expanded. We now have offices in Delhi, Bangalore, Pune and Hyderabad as well," he corrected her politely, but not without displaying a hint of scorn.

"Sorry, my mistake. And congratulations Bobby! I am glad Blu is doing so well," Zoya answered with a genuinely warm smile. Though it was hard to miss a certain archness in her demeanour.

Bobby turned towards Richard and added, "And recently

sir, we just completed redoing the interiors of Mr. Ashok's new corporate office in Cuffe Parade. I am sure you know..."

"Oh yes, I know Ashok very well," Richard interrupted him.

Bobby was extremely proud of his elite private education and liked to drop names. He smiled constantly and spoke with a carefully cultivated drawl, another of his private school affectations. Even his laughter was light, frothy and measured. He had a habit of throwing his head back and laughing every few minutes, as if he found the world rather amusing. The whole look was carefully crafted to exude cool, effortless style but his small shifty eyes gave him away. They would dart quickly from side to side as he spoke, as if they were constantly sizing you up.

Pointing at the woman standing next to Bobby, Zoya said, "Richard, this is Sophie D'mello. Sophie has just come on board and handles marketing." The woman immediately extended her card and smiled coquettishly. She seemed to be in her early twenties, dark, slim and rather short. She wore a deep wine red ruffled top, a fitted grey skirt and six-inch black stilettos. Her shoulder-length hair seemed to have been straightened and had been expertly layered with blonde highlights, which shone brightly in the airport lighting. She would toss these tresses back from time to time. "Blu Tulip was the first company I worked with. And Bobby here was my team head," Zoya explained to Richard.

"Besides leading the team, I headed the creative group at that time as well," Bobby added with grave solemnity.

"And Bobby, this is Richard–," Zoya started to introduce him, when Bobby interrupted her again.

"Ah you needn't bother, Zoya. I know Mr. Wiseman."

Seeing Richard's surprise, he added, "Sir, we met at the convention this March. I attended your talk on 'Unleashing Innovation'. Wonderful talk, it enlightened me on so many levels. If I may add, I have looked at my work with a new eye."

"Thank you. You are very kind," Richard said, smiling a little, and casually glanced at his watch.

There was a long pause. Bobby was still looking at Richard, as if he expected something more in return for his kind words. But Richard kept quiet. Finally, when the lull seemed to end the conversation all together, Bobby turned back to Zoya.

"So Zoya, how have you been?" Without waiting for her to reply, he turned towards Richard and added, "Mr. Wiseman, we had taken in Zoya when she was fresh out of school.

"Lively girl. She had nice prospects. But she left our company too soon," he added with a sigh. Then turning towards her, he added, "Had you stayed on with us, Zoya, you would have been here today."

"I am here today, Bobby." Zoya smiled, a little fixedly. That prompted yet another of Bobby's characteristic laughs.

"That's a nice one, I mean here today with me at the exhibition," he added. Then addressing Richard, he continued, "I am proud to say we are one of the few Indian companies that has been formally invited to participate in the

INDEX Interior Design Show here. It's a very prestigious exhibition. In fact, it is one of the top exhibitions in this region."

"That's great! Congratulations," Richard answered.

Then sensing that that was all Richard was going to muster, Bobby again turned his attention to Zoya.

"So what's up with you, girl? Still painting children's books? And how's the gallery work going... er, is it still going?" he asked Zoya condescendingly.

"Yes, it's going well, Bobby. Both my work with children's books and gallery assignments. Thank you for asking," she answered, with a slight edge in her voice.

"In fact, I think she's doing really well. We are in the midst of negotiating a rather expensive deal," Richard said.

Both Zoya and Bobby looked at Richard with surprise.

"We're planning to exhibit Zoya's art at all our office locations in India. Actually, we just went through a major restructuring exercise and I think changing the look of our offices in line with our new ethos maybe a very good idea. Zoya's work captures the new brand ethos really well," Richard added.

"In that case, you must give us an opportunity to present our work. I'm sure our ideas can–," Bobby started.

"Thanks, I am sure they are wonderful. But I think for now, Zoya's work will do. I'm looking at around four to six artworks for each office and it might take a substantial amount of time to complete the entire exercise. How much time do you think it will take, Zoya?"

Zoya was staring at him with her mouth slightly open

WHAT YOU SEEK IS SEEKING YOU

but sensing Bobby's gaze, she regained her composure. She smiled, but still didn't answer.

"Well that's great! Good going, Zoya," Bobby filled in, unable to mask the surprise in his voice. Then, with an air of grave concern, he turned to Richard, "But if I might suggest, for an exercise of this magnitude, it might not be feasible to bank on just one artist." Glancing back at her, he said, "Please don't mind my comment, Zoya. It's not personal."

"Of course not!" she mumbled.

Turning towards Richard, he continued, "As I was saying, we have collaborations with leading artists and can suggest a range of work that will go well with your new look. I could come to your office to discuss it.

"In fact, if you have a few minutes, I could show you the catalogues right now. Get those 2013-2014 catalogues, sweetheart," he quickly gestured to Sophie. Sophie, who was so far happily playing the wallflower, immediately transformed into a beehive of activity. She bent down to shuffle about in her oversized Gucci bag when Bobby interrupted her.

"Sophie, forget the hard copies. What's your smartphone for? Open the catalogues on our website," he said hastily, with a slight hint of irritation in his characteristic drawl.

"We'll discuss it, Bobby. But some other time, maybe. Right now I am not in a mood to discuss business," Richard nodded with a smile, but his tone carried an air of finality, signaling a close to the topic.

Bobby acquiesced quickly, "Sure, Mr. Wiseman."

Zoya wondered how Richard managed to cut people down

to size in only one bite. Putting an end to the boisterous Bobby was never an easy task. As if on cue, Bobby once again turned his attention to her.

"So where are you off to, Zoya?"

She seemed to have become his rallying point. Whenever there was a lull in conversation, Bobby would wave the 'Zoya flag' to start off yet another discussion. That was Bobby for you. Persistent like a bulldog, he wouldn't stop until he had made a sale.

But she wisely kept her thoughts to herself and replied, "Turkey."

"Oh, planning to spend your New Year's there! Good, good, keep it up. One of the perks of working from home – extended vacations," he said, laughing at his own joke.

"Actually Bobby, I'm traveling for work. Going to attend a Sufi Dance festival. It's–," Zoya began, but was interrupted by Bobby yet again.

"Achha? Good, so you are still continuing with your spiritual stuff," he drawled sarcastically. "I always say, Mr. Wiseman, don't lose sight of God. If you keep Him in mind, then He'll keep you in mind. In fact, I follow a regular set of practices myself. I am very particular about starting my day with prayer. And I fast every Saturday. And no meat or alcohol on Tuesdays."

"Interesting! That's a nice barter system with God. *Keep Him in mind so that He keeps you in mind.* Thanks, I'll remember that," Richard said with a close-lipped smile.

"Oh, just one of the things I picked up from my experiences in life," Bobby said in a wistful tone. "So Zoya, keep the faith,

girl. This spiritual stuff is good for you. Don't lose hope yet,"
he said, leaning forward to pat her gently on the shoulder.

By this time, Zoya's calm composure was beginning to
crack up. She had a sudden vision of picking up Sophie's
Gucci bag and hitting the patronizing Bobby on his head.
"The nerve of this man. It's been eight years since I left Blu
and he still has the cheek to tell me how I am supposed to
feel," she fumed.

Just then, Richard piped in, "I think she has more than her
faith keeping her up. Her spirituality goes beyond practices
and infuses her life. This is evident when you see her art
as well. Her paintings have this crisp, reverberating energy
that's infectious. Very authentic."

Zoya thought to herself, "Oh God! Now what's wrong?
At first he didn't want to even venture beyond a few words
and now he swoops in like Tarzan every time Bobby shoots a
dart." She was getting tired of these men telling her how she
was feeling and validating her experiences. She wondered
why men can't just let women be.

She saw Richard glancing in her direction, but she quickly
averted her gaze. She looked around for an excuse to end
this discussion about her supposed state of being, and luckily
found one, just in time.

"Sorry to interrupt, but I think we'd better leave. They
have announced boarding, Richard," she said with an extra
sweet smile.

"Oh yes! Indeed. It was nice meeting you, Bobby and…
uh, Sophie. Have a safe flight back," Richard smiled and
shook their hands.

Realizing there was no way to continue, Bobby plunged in for the final act. "The pleasure was mine, sir. I'll give you a call once you are back in Mumbai to discuss our way ahead."

"Sure. Call my office to set up an appointment," Richard answered.

Ms. Wallflower stood there smiling a little nervously, waiting for her cue from Bobby.

"It was nice catching up with you Bobby. Take care. And nice to meet you, Sophie." Without waiting for a response, Zoya bent down to pick up her bag.

Sophie started to mumble something, but seeing that nobody was paying any attention, picked up her bag and turned towards her boss expectantly.

Glad to be finally done, Zoya turned and walked resolutely towards the boarding gates with Richard following behind. Suddenly, he leaned forward and whispered in her ear, "Was that the jerk of the highest order you were mentioning earlier?"

Zoya turned back and gave him a steely smile and answered in a saccharin tone, "I think we're late. We should hurry." She continued ahead, feeling furious with them all, but more so with herself for letting this affect her so much. Despite all the changes she thought she had made within herself, there was still a bit of the 23-year-old Zoya within her, who got upset whenever someone even briefly commented on her abilities. Had she not changed at all?

Richard then wisely kept quiet the entire way back.

Once they were settled in their seats, with Zoya once again

taking the window seat, she pressed the button for the flight attendant and asked for a blanket.

"Are you all right? If you're feeling cold, we can turn off the AC," Richard ventured, raising his hand towards the knob.

"I'm perfectly fine. No need to turn off the AC," she answered quickly, smiling fixedly and turned her head towards the window, staring intently at the ground below. Since the plane was still awaiting clearance, Richard wondered what she was finding so interesting outside.

"Are you sure you're okay?" he attempted again. He seemed to have set off a ticking time-bomb for she immediately turned on him.

"Well, until now I thought I was. But if you care to venture a different opinion and enlighten me on my true feelings, then please go ahead, Mr. Wiseman," she said pointedly, her eyes blazing.

"I'm sorry. What do you mean?"

Just then the flight attendant returned with a red blanket.

"It's nothing. Let it be," Zoya answered dismissively, wrapping the blanket around her tightly.

"It is something. You seem disturbed."

"There you go again, telling me how I feel."

"Miss Rahman, I have known you only for a few hours and I'm still trying to figure you out. So if you could come to the point and tell me what's wrong, then I can help you that much quicker."

"Well, that's precisely the point. I don't need your help… or anybody else's for that matter."

"Excuse me?" he stared at her, not comprehending what she meant.

"I mean what was that rescue act all about?"

"What rescue act?" he asked, raising his arms in bewilderment.

"I think it's best if we don't pursue this topic of conversation any further. We will reach our respective destinations in some time and be on our separate ways. So, no point arguing for the next few hours, and it's nothing really. I don't even remember much of what was said back there," Zoya retorted, ending her speech with a pointed sigh.

"Can I also have a part in deciding whether or not this topic merits any further conversation? Now that you have accused me of rescuing you, I think I deserve to discover the finer details of my heroic act," Richard said, a little exasperated.

"The act where you were planning to so generously display my art in your office. And vouching for me; talking about how spiritually infused I was; how things beyond my faith were keeping me up; how my work was authentic and reverberating with energy."

"Wow! For someone who does not claim to remember much, you have not missed anything," he stated dryly. "And getting back to my act, it was no act. Really!" he added with a fixed smile. "I meant every word I said. I like your work. And believe it or not, I have seen quite a lot of art to be able to make a decent observation about it. Yes, your kind of work is a little too dramatic for me, but I get a good vibe when I see it. I was actually considering a deal with you."

"Oh please, save the excuses!" she said derisively.

"And I really think you should expose your work to a bigger market. I can help you with that," he added.

"Thanks! But I'm very happy with the way things are. I am doing perfectly fine without 'help'," she glowered back.

"I don't get it. What are you mad about? The fact that I praised your work in front of your ex-boss or that I said I can help you?" he asked, even more bewildered than before.

"Well, for starters, I like my life and the way it functions. I wouldn't want to change anything. And so I don't care what anybody else thinks about it."

"Well then, you are right. I do disapprove of your way of life," he said.

"Excuse me!" she said incredulously, his last comment rousing her to meet his gaze.

"No, you are not excused! You cannot drag unsuspecting and unwilling strangers into long-winding conversations on topics they have no clue about and then excuse yourself when you want to. If you talk with so much passion and fervor, then you should have the temerity to listen with the same openness.

"And yes, I do disapprove of your life. I disapprove of the way you keep quiet when silly people dismember your work, and you let them get away with it. I disapprove of the way you talk big about realizing your potential and painting your life on a large canvas, yet choose to cloister your talent from the rest of the world and even from yourself, by not trying hard enough.

"I disapprove of the way you talk about the oneness, yet

bristle at the very idea of accepting help from somebody.

"So tell me, Miss Rahman, is it not your ego that's preventing you from accepting my help? You said it right before; the ways of the ego are indeed subtle," he said, looking away and shaking his head in disbelief.

Zoya, who had hoped to end the discussion, suddenly couldn't contain herself. As soon as he finished speaking, her cheeks flushed pink and she said, "Well, now that you have accused me of being egotistic, let me answer your accusations.

"I don't care what people think of me. So if a man like Bobby comes up to me and tries to belittle my work, I simply choose not to respond. I know my own value. So there is no need for a third party to defend it either.

"Secondly, if I choose to not run after money or become a hotshot CEO in the corporate world, I don't see how it counters my philosophy of living my life to the full. I don't measure my life in those terms."

This last part, he was sure, was pointed at him.

"Thirdly, I do see the oneness in all. Hence, I do not like to inconvenience anyone on my behalf. So I prefer to take care of my own matters. I don't see how that amounts to me indulging my ego. So there, I hope I have answered your concerns," she said, pointedly.

Richard, who had been listening to her quietly, and who had always prided himself on his cool and unruffled manner even amid the tensest of negotiations, blurted out, "No, you haven't."

"Oh, so you have something more to say," she reacted.

"No, merely a counter observation to your explanations," he answered with a forced attempt at calmness.

"Please go on, I'm most eager to hear them," she said coolly, though her expression said otherwise. Her heart was pounding and the anger steadily building up inside was threatening to engulf her.

Richard was at that moment battling the conflicting voices in his head. One part of him, the usually dominant one, was telling him to keep calm and stop speaking. After all, she was just a stranger he had met at the airport. She was someone he had not even liked in the beginning. Moreover, she had a right to live her life her way. The other part of him was itching to tell her how he really felt. Damn it, she had a right to know the truth, even if it was his version.

He chose the latter.

"Well, to your first explanation, if you didn't care about what people thought or said about you, we wouldn't be having this conversation.

"Second, you are not choosing to run after money or big contracts not because you don't see any value in them; it's because you are scared of what they represent. They represent a plunge into the real, gritty, big world out there, with your work open to censure and ridicule; facing your fears of not being perfect; and the possibility of seeing your romanticized opinions about life, that you have cultivated with so much love and affection, biting the dust. It poses a real danger of plunging even deeper into yourself to thresh out the real YOU.

"Third, you do not accept help not because you are

independent, but because accepting help means revealing your vulnerable side. It means admitting the fact that you don't know it all and that you can't do it all.

"In other words, you are playing it safe. But all that you're escaping is you. And yet I commend you. Because you are also incredibly brave to still go ahead amidst all your contradictions to try to be true to yourself. To still be kind, wonderful and gentle with all you encounter, to retain your wide-eyed wonder about life. But unless you acknowledge these fears, there is no moving ahead, there is no honoring the spirit that is pulsating in you."

She started to say something. But he raised his palm. "No, you don't have to defend yourself again. We're not here to prove each other right or wrong. Nor am I here to hurt your feelings. I have merely offered my honest opinion on what I truly felt. And yes, I may be totally wrong. But I say things as I see them. So if you see any sense in what I've said, good. And if you think that all I have said is rubbish, you are free to ignore it," Richard said, as if closing the topic.

She looked at him for a long moment with an expression of mingled astonishment and mortification, and then abruptly closed her eyes.

He was taken aback as he had never seen anyone close their eyes in the middle of an argument. He wondered if that meant the discussion was over.

She opened her eyes after a while and spoke slowly, as if measuring and weighing each word before uttering it.

"To refute you outright or completely dismiss your opinions would be tantamount to dismissing this moment.

Plus the surge of emotion and candor that you have shown to someone who was a complete stranger just a few hours back does merit a more considered response. I will certainly reflect on all you have said, but for now I think I must keep my counsel."

With that, Zoya turned away and looked out of the window. The sky was empty and stark blue, bereft of any clouds, deeply contrasting with her state of mind, which was right now a snarling river of turmoil, her emotions threatening to spill over. And the last thing she wanted was for him to see her cry.

Richard stared at her for a few moments and started to say something, but then held back and slowly opened his laptop. Within minutes, he seemed to have forgotten the interlude and was deeply engrossed in his work.

Zoya closed her eyes and tried to calm her mind. But doing that never worked when she had conflicting emotions to quell. Her thoughts always resurfaced, dampening her spirit, especially when she was in the middle of something happy. She knew she had to deal with them, one by one. So she decided resolutely that before going to sleep that night, she would thrash out all that he had said, dissect each statement with surgical precision, reason them out with her conscience and then be done with them.

With that, she took out her book and started to read, and was soon immersed in it.

Time passed quickly. Soon they descended with the beautiful evening skyline of Istanbul rising fast to engulf them. He closed his laptop and for a moment, sat there quietly. Then he turned to look towards her and smiled. "So, our journey is coming to an end," he sighed.

"Just this part. The rest will continue," she said and smiled back.

He nodded his head, but didn't say anything in return.

There was a long uncomfortable pause. Neither spoke for a long time.

Zoya broke the silence first. "It was nice to meet you, Richard. I hope you have a great conference. And hopefully you'll find some time to sightsee as well. Istanbul is supposed to be beautiful."

"Yes, beautiful indeed," he said, looking at her for a long moment.

He adjusted his glasses and rummaged in his coat pocket. "Here's my card. Do let me know how the festival goes."

She looked at it for a few moments before putting it in her bag.

Neither spoke again for a while.

"Uh, may I have your card? I'm serious about the paintings. My office will give you a call, if you don't mind," he said.

"Yeah, sure! Here," she said with feigned indifference and took a slim card from her bag.

He looked at it, turning it over.

One side was plain matt ivory, with her details neatly printed in blue. The other showed a painting of a peacock's plume that was a riot of colors.

"One of my earlier paintings," she explained.

The flight landed with a small thump and the momentum pinned them to their seats. Soon, there was a steady hum of conversation and beeping cellphones and life began to return to normal.

He helped her lower her camera and luggage from the overhead rack and pulled down his own bag.

There was a short wait until the doors opened and the stream of humans began to eagerly clamber out of the plane. Zoya moved ahead quickly, gracefully maneuvering her bag through the narrow aisle. But her fingers gripped the handle tensely. He followed her slowly, feeling low. It was as if the last act of a vigorous full-throated opera had ended with a squeak. Within minutes, they were inside the Ataturk airport that was bustling like a market. It was nothing compared to the glamour of Dubai, but the energy here was more palpable.

She turned towards him with her hand outstretched.

"So, I'll take your leave now. It was an eventful flight, one I think I will remember for a long time," she added, smiling.

"My feelings exactly," he agreed.

"How are you planning to get to your hotel? Can I drop you someplace?" he inquired. "I'll have an office car."

"Oh don't worry. I can manage," she answered quickly. "But thanks for the offer," she added as an afterthought.

They stood there awkwardly for a moment, both silent.

"I think I'll use the washroom before I collect my luggage." With that, Zoya gave a swift nod and quickly turned towards the washroom.

## Bringing It to Life: Messages from Chapter Ten – Appreciating the Benefits of Receiving

### The Storyline

Richard tries to help Zoya, first by protecting her interests in the encounter with Bobbi Oberoi and then by giving her his perspective on her reaction. Zoya, however, sees his offer to buy her paintings as undermining her ability to fend for herself, and becomes defensive.

### Messages

*"And now you ask in your heart, 'How shall we distinguish that which is pleasurable from that which is not?'*
*Go to your fields and your gardens, and you shall learn that it is the pleasure of the bee to gather honey of the flower,*
*But it is also the pleasure of the flower to yield its honey to the bee.*
*For to the bee, a flower is a fountain of life,*
*And to the flower, a bee is a messenger of love,*
*And to both, bee and flower, the giving and the receiving of pleasure is a need and an ecstasy."*

– Khalil Gibran

### Reflect on the following questions:

- Do you graciously accept a compliment, feedback or a gift?

- Do you feel that receiving is a sign of weakness?

- Do you ask for help when you need it?

- Do you worry about paying back after receiving?

- Is independence more valuable to you than interdependence?

- Do you receive graciously and pay it back by doing a kind deed for someone else?

- Do you believe it takes a stronger person to accept help?

- Do you worry someone will take advantage of you if you accept help?

Giving is perceived to have a greater moral significance than receiving; in fact, we often view receiving as a reflection of some kind of inadequacy on the part of the receiver, but this is not so. Receiving is as important as giving – listening, witnessing, observing and paying attention are all part of receiving – and we cannot be truly spiritually until we are as open to receiving as we are to giving.

Some people feel they are weak or have failed when they ask for help, as if they don't have the capacity to achieve their goals themselves. However, we all have strengths and weaknesses. If we focus on our strengths and work on our weaknesses, we can achieve much more. If we seek help in areas where we are not particularly accomplished, we benefit a lot and give other people a chance to give – and being able to give is truly a blessing. Some people are good givers who feel that giving is a joy. They are right in thinking so. However, to only give and not receive will not hold balance because, as you *give*, you also *get*. When one talks about receiving in terms of tangible resources, then it also means that one must carefully use those resources. Only giving will deplete resources and thus, one who *gives* must also *receive* from others, so that the act of giving and receiving is always sustained well and replenished. This is akin to the process of Nature where we see the balance between life and birth, giving and acquiring in all its forms. When somebody tells you that you've done a good job, instead of dismissing it, politely say, "Thank you very much." Such courtesies always build lasting relations between people.

We live in a society where independence is valued as a positive attribute. However, it is almost impossible for most of us to live and work in isolation or independently all our lives because in every society, human beings need to co-exist. Each of us, at some point, have been interdependent, which is more rewarding at different junctures in life. Being interdependent is not a sign of weakness; in fact, it shows a person's ability to co-exist and co-operate with other beings to accomplish endeavors.

Some people fear that if they accept something, they will owe something in return. We all practice reciprocity at some point in our lives. For instance, if you receive help from someone, it's natural to want to help them in some way. There's nothing wrong with that. If someone offers to help you, accept it. One day, you'll have a chance to return the favor, but it shouldn't be a burden.

Azim was speaking to a group from the World Presidents' Organization in Hyderabad, India, and was describing the concept of giving when one of the members shared an experience with him. He was once a part of the leadership of a round table club and gave a big cheque from the club to Mother Teresa. She took the cheque, looked him in the eye and thanked him for his generous donation. She then put her hand on his shoulder and after a moment said something that really affected him. She said, "Never forget to thank the people who allow you to serve them." In other words, thank those people who receive help.

Sometimes you may feel that people who give have ulterior motives and want to take advantage of you. In general, though, unless you have doubts about a person's integrity or authenticity, if they are giving, you should receive the gift with grace. If you find later that they want to take advantage of you, then end your relationship.

It is also important to give and receive within a team. Too often, the corporate world forces individuals to strive and show their personal strengths. However, accepting help from others and crediting them for it is not a sign of weakness. It takes a stronger person to take help than not to take help.

Receiving means being open to feedback, suggestions, guidance, mentoring and coaching. If a CEO is open to receiving feedback, then he/she is in a better position to improve things in the business. You don't have to implement all you receive, but keep the benefit in mind. Receiving lightens your load and makes things easier.

*Challenge yourself with the following 'How to' exercises:*

1) RECEIVE with grace whether it's a compliment, feedback, constructive criticism or a gift. If you accept something with grace, you show genuine appreciation to the giver.

2) WHEN someone gives something with good intent, receive it, even if it's not what you really want.

3) ASK for help when you need it. Start small if you find it difficult to receive and then progress from there.

4) REMIND yourself each day that it takes a confident person to receive, therefore receive things with an open heart and mind.

5) AVOID keeping score when giving or receiving: when you receive something, don't worry about giving something in return. Yes, there will be those who only give because they expect returns; but there are many others who give because they only want to give – people who like you or already feel you are giving to them in other ways – a friendship, lending a patient ear, moral support and so on.

6) RECEIVING is important, since you wouldn't be where you are if you weren't already receiving – for instance, knowledge from a teacher, encouragement from friends, support from family and so on.

7) RECEIVE AND PAY IT FORWARD, even at times when you cannot do it directly. A friend of Azim recently passed away at the age of 58. He had helped Azim in editing this book, giving unconditional, insightful feedback. So, Azim found ways to help the family cope with the enormous loss.

# Chapter Eleven

# Transforming Negative Ego into Positive Pride

*"Give up the drop. Become the ocean."*

– Rumi

When Zoya came back, Richard had left.

Immigration took another hour before she was free to leave the airport.

She hailed a cab and gave the address of the B&B she had booked online. According to her GPS, it would take her 35 to 40 minutes to get to her location.

As soon as she settled in, she called her parents to tell them she had arrived. Her father answered the phone. As usual, he answered in monosyllables, but sounded relieved and then handed over the phone to her mother.

After assuring her mother that she had reached Istanbul safe and sound, and that she would send them a message after reaching her B&B, Zoya finally leaned back and sighed.

She was 32 and lived in her own rental apartment. She was used to traveling alone but her mother still fussed over her, as if she were Bambi. In her heart, she understood where all that concern came from and the fact that she was a mother, only heightened her fears.

The cab snaked its way through the busy streets. After a few miles, the road ahead widened. The spectacle of the sea on the one side, glistening in the evening sun, and the skyline on the other, took Zoya's breath away. But this idyllic scene could not capture her attention for long. Her mind kept drifting elsewhere.

She kept replaying her last conversation with Richard. "Ways of the ego are subtle indeed?"

What cheek! What if she chose to live like this? She loved her freedom. Not everybody had to join the rat race to feel fulfilled.

"Like Richard had joined," she told herself, emphatically.

He actually had the gall to accuse her of being scared, scared of the "big" world – the one over which he lorded as the CEO. But what about the little world– – the one with the people who really mattered? The only significant relationship he had was with himself. Nobody else seemed to matter. But then a tiny voice told her she was being a little unfair, when he had seemed to care. He cared enough to listen. He cared enough to argue on her behalf.

So what? He was still so aloof, so inaccessible. He couldn't bear to open himself up. And he called love a 'risky proposition'. So, who was the scared one now, Mr. CEO?

Just then her cab driver spoke, "Madam, that's the Blue Mosque, on your left."

"Uhh, what?" But by the time she looked out of the window, they had already passed it.

"Damn! How could I miss it?" she thought dejectedly.

"So much for being in the *moment,*" the tiny voice inside her head piped in again.

Well, it was true. Where was all that awareness she talked about? If an incident with a complete stranger had the power to unnerve her, what was the point of talking big about being in the *present moment,* or *being aware?*

So maybe he was right, after all. Maybe she was all talk and no substance. Maybe she really was scared of venturing out, scared of living amidst the Bhushan Oberois of the world.

Maybe she was terrified. But then the tiny voice butted in again, "Don't forget, he complimented you as well, he called you authentic... and wonderful and kind."

Ughhhh, no, no, no... that wasn't where her thoughts were supposed to wander. She had to be present here, right now, in her cab, in Istanbul, in this gorgeous street, which smelled incredible by the way.

She peered out quickly, just in time to see a street hawker selling some vegetables and some strange-looking meat roasting on a spit. Her stomach grumbled in response.

The cab had now left the main road and was entering tiny cobbled lanes with neat little flower boxes lining the homes. There were people sitting at cafes and idling over coffee.

Her companion on all her travel sojourns, the Lonely Planet travel guide, had recommended her a B&B. It was supposed to be safe, moderately cheap and centrally located.

Her cab skirted a couple of narrow lanes, and stopped abruptly in front of a quaint, small building that turned out to be her B&B.

It was owned by two European women. And the book had further highlighted that it was just a 15-minute walk from the Blue Mosque.

The cabdriver helped her down with her luggage. She knocked on the main door but realized that it was open. She saw a little girl at the door with a mass of red curls. The girl looked at her and especially at her clothes with an unwavering gaze.

"Hi, is your mommy at home?"

The girl ran back inside and appeared a little later with an older woman, presumably her mother. She had the same head of curls, but a lot more orange.

"Hi, I'm Zoya Rahman. I booked a room. Online…"

"Oh yes, yes, come in. We were expecting you a lot sooner."

"My flight was delayed."

"No problem. Come in dear." She helped Zoya in with her luggage.

It was a pretty little place, everything dainty and neat. The walls were covered in creamy ivory and everything, from the sofas to the tablecloth, had a fuzzy pink paisley print.

It was as if you had walked into a warm strawberry cake. There was a small foyer that led to the kitchen on the left. On the right was a tiny room which probably served as their office. Another passage adjacent to the kitchen probably led to other rooms. But the most interesting highlight was the curved staircase right in front of the main door.

After taking her passport and booking details, Myra, one of the owners, led her up the stairs to her room. Her partner, Janice, was out at the time.

The room, like the rest of the place, was small and very old-world with a queen-size bed and a slim wooden wardrobe. There was a tiny little chair by the window, again covered in pink paisley.

There was just about enough leg-room to open the wardrobe or get to the attached washroom.

"This is your room. The bathroom is there. She pointed to a door. Breakfast is from seven to nine. And if you need anything, just call me or Janice."

"Thanks! I think I'll just freshen up and settle down for an early dinner. Can you give me directions to the nearest café or restaurant?"

"Why don't you join us for dinner tonight? It will be ready

in an hour," Myra offered.

Zoya agreed readily, and thanked her profusely. The prospect of venturing out into a new city after a long and rather eventful day was not very appealing to her anyway.

After a quick wash and a text to her mother, she put her phone on charge and went downstairs.

The dinner was a simple but wholesome affair. Janice had returned and all four of them, including little Mia, chattered noisily, pausing only to eat.

There was a large loaf of freshly baked bread, a delightful concoction of cottage cheese and vegetables marinated in a fragrant red sauce, fried chicken, Waldorf salad and a tall pitcher of iced tea.

The food had improved Zoya's mood and she was back to her old animated self, enjoying every moment with her new acquaintances.

Mia was fascinated by Zoya's bangles and kept watching them, as they jingled on her arms when she ate. She was thrilled when Zoya happily handed them to her.

Zoya liked children. It was so easy to be yourself among them. They were so full of wonder and joy and easy camaraderie. There was no hint of malice or pretense.

Moreover, it was difficult not to adore Mia, what with her swinging red curls and throbbing curiosity, evident in her sparkling blue eyes that reminded Zoya of another pair of blue eyes – eyes that turned an icy grey in anger.

*"Oh God, why am I thinking of him again? And when did I notice his eye color? This is not right. No, it's not. And I'm sure he has conveniently forgotten me and our episode and moved on to his*

*big conference, while I'm wasting my time thinking about him,"* she thought, feeling even more dejected.

Zoya shook her head, firmly pushing back those stupid, agonizing thoughts, and got back to Mia. But within 15 to 20 minutes, she began to yawn. She decided to call it a night and after thanking them for dinner, went back to her room.

She plunked herself on the bed and checked her phone. There were a couple of work emails and four messages, one of them from a new number.

It was Richard, checking on whether she had reached her hotel. She got up to re-check. Yes, it was Richard!

*"Hmm, so he does seem to remember basic courtesy,"* she thought aloud, secretly pleased with his message. She read it a number of times, as if still in disbelief that the message was from Richard. Her immediate thought was to reply but her tiny inner voice popped up again, telling her that a response was not needed since he had acted unreasonably.

She told herself, "Why should what he said bother me so much *now*? That moment has passed. I didn't spare him either; painting him like a cold, emotionless person. And anyway, decency demands that I reply to his message. After all, we are mature individuals who can agree to disagree. Moreover, this will show him that I don't let my ego get the better of me."

However, that last thought did reek of some ego. *What was the need to prove something if you were so devoid of ego?* the tiny voice whispered again.

*Too much thinking, again!* Zoya resolutely sent him a casual message that she had arrived and hoped he too had settled in. She then quickly brushed her teeth and dressed for bed. Tomorrow was going to be a long day again. This was her only day to experience Istanbul before she drove to Konya for the festival.

She fell asleep as soon as her head hit the pillow, forgetting the promise she had made earlier to resolve her conflict.

## Bringing It to Life: Messages from Chapter Eleven – Transforming Negative Ego into Positive Pride

### The Storyline

The tiny voice inside Zoya keeps talking to her, reminding her that Richard is trying to help her. This tiny voice is trying to override her ego.

### Messages

*"I do not know what I may appear to the world, but to myself I seem to have been only like a boy playing on the sea-shore, and diverting myself now and then in finding a smoother pebble or a prettier shell than ordinary, whilst the great ocean of truth lay all undiscovered before me."*

— Isaac Newton

### Reflect on the following questions:

- Do you often compare yourself to others? If so, why?

- In a typical day, what do you spend most of your time thinking about: the past? the future? something else? Reflect on why your focus is where it is.

- What does ego mean to you?

- Do you often feel other people are egotistical?

- Do you get defensive when given feedback?

- Do you get annoyed easily when working in a team?

- Do you want to always stand out and be recognized?

- Do you feel the need to point out how you're kinder, richer, smarter, better or more successful than others?

- Do you treat your partner, child and colleague as less superior?

One of the biggest challenges you will face on your journey to seek your life purpose is the battle to overcome the self (ego). Ego takes you away from your innate gifts: your special talents and abilities. It focuses more on power outside of you instead of the power *within*. You become defensive and self-centered. The ego is subtle and difficult to see. You need to observe your own thoughts and develop awareness of yourself in order to catch the ego in the act.

Fear, judgment, emotional baggage, lack of teamwork, inferiority and superiority complexes and lack of productivity all stem from negative ego. You think of yourself all the time. Everything that is discussed around you, you process it in ways that might benefit or hurt you personally. You are closed to others' ideas; only *your* ideas matter. Whenever you receive constructive feedback, you become defensive as if you are always right. There is potential for growth. The antidote is to recognize that it's not all about *you*.

How much does negative ego cost your company? It leads to lack of teamwork, promotes fear, creates a scarcity mindset wherein there simply isn't enough to go around. This fosters an antagonistic environment that affects both work and profitability.

Some analysts estimate that ego accounts for 6 percent in lost revenue. If this is true, then the annual "cost of ego" would translate to nearly $1.1 billion for the average Fortune 500 Company. Negative ego can also lead us to turn our back on innovation and make other regrettable mistakes. Here are some examples that demonstrate that ego could have played a part:

- This is how William Orton, President of Western Union Telegraph company, responded to Alexander Graham Bell's offer to sell the patent for the telephone for $100,000: "What use could this company have for an electrical toy?"

- Robert Uihlein, CEO of Schlitz Brewing Company, was able to drastically reduce his beer's brewing time by replacing the barley in the formulation with corn syrup. This move got the product to market faster, which resulted in better short-term profits. However, it was a failure in the long term after customers realized that the new formula tasted terrible, and quickly broke down into a mucus-like, thick consistency. Schlitz's fall from grace was quick.

Just when you think you have conquered your ego, it returns through the back door. Therefore, be vigilant about it. The best way to maintain vigilance is through constant awareness. Usually, if you feel at peace, you are beyond your ego. When uneasiness sets in, it is a sign that the ego is creeping in again. The sooner you catch yourself reacting and the sooner you change course, the better your outcome will be. Whenever you feel you are acting negatively, check yourself and ask if you are acting in alignment with your highest self. This will prevent you from falling prey to negative ego and motivate you to work from a place of positive pride. When we vigilantly observe ourselves, the light of that awareness starts to starve the ego. Bereft of negativity, gossip and blame, the ego starts to dissolve and disintegrate.

Remember the words of Jiddu Krishnamurti: "When the mind goes beyond the thought of 'the me', the experiencer, the observer, the thinker, then there is a possibility of a happiness that is incorruptible."

Positive pride, on the other hand, is good. It means you believe in yourself, in your capacity; you believe you're gifted, and that's okay, as long as you use that pride to make the world a better place, to create positive change and live a wonderful life.

You were brought into this world for success, not failure. If you don't believe in yourself, nobody else will. We admire the glory of the stars, the abundance of the ocean and the beauty of the changing seasons. These attributes spring from a universal benevolence. With positive pride and self-esteem, we can value these gifts and use them to make a difference. There is a story among the Sufis about an eagle flying high in the sky, admiring his own beauty, and "looking down" on things on the ground. These egotistical thoughts are abruptly terminated when an arrow strikes the bird and it falls to the ground. The eagle can't believe it has been hit, especially by a piece of metal. Then it sees its feathers on the ground and exclaims, "It is the feathers that made me fly high in the sky and they are the same feathers that make me fall to the ground." Moral of the story: we all have positive pride that can help us soar the skies of success but we also have ego that can destroy us.

Keep the bigger picture in mind. Have clear long- and short-term goals, which will create accountability in your life. Say no to unimportant activities. Write out your personal mission statement, long-term (one to three years) and short-term (one to three months) goals. Read them every morning and night.

Here's a example of a personal mission statement:

"Shine my light and inspire others to shine their light. To be a loving father, husband, son and human being."

People with pride and self-esteem obviously value their own talents, but do not remain centered on them. They are willing to accept and appreciate and are valued for who they are. Their self-esteem places them in high positions; they get good results and their involvement with people around them earns them respect and genuine admiration.

### Challenge yourself with the following 'How to' exercises:

1) BE AWARE that you have an ego, even if you don't think you do – the humblest of people have ego, not only those who are arrogant. Awareness is the starting point of transformation. The acid test is to ask yourself: Am I happy and at peace?

   If the answer is yes, you have transformed ego. If the answer is a mixed bag of yes and no, there is work to be done.

2) ASK people close to you what they think about your

behavior, actions, etc. Do they see a subtle ego in you? Be objective about what other people think about your behavior and how it affects them.

3) EGO takes you away from the present moment because while you're doing a task, your ego will say things like: "I'm not making enough money, I'm not getting the recognition I deserve, I need to pay my bills, I'm not happy, I don't have enough." Be aware of this and try to refocus on the task at hand.

4) EVALUATE how many of your thoughts are ego-driven and how many are driven by the desire to make a difference in the lives of others. Replace ego-driven thoughts with actions that make a difference to one and all.

5) CATCH yourself when you get frustrated, because your ego is putting the focus on you and wanting everyone else to comply.

6) REMEMBER that no one achieves greatness alone. Everything you achieve is connected in some way with help and support from others – be it your team, family, friends, supporters or customers.

7) VALUE diversity: value the difference in others and see their strengths. Your openness to look at and appreciate the strengths of others, rather than being too self-centered, reflects positive pride. It reminds you that someone else's strength does not diminish your own strengths.

8) EXPRESS gratitude for the many things you have – your five senses, your intelligence, health, family, friends, even life itself.

# Chapter Twelve

# Transcending Fear

*"There is no illusion greater than fear."*

— Lao Tzu

Richard was in bed, reading the book Zoya had gifted him, when he heard his phone beep. It was Zoya informing him that she had arrived, and politely asking if he too had settled in.

But her overall tone was cool and crisp, maybe even a little curt, or was he just imagining this?

It confirmed his fears though. She was still upset. And who wouldn't be, after getting such a long drawn-out lecture, one that was dripping with judgment and censure, and that too from a complete stranger? He really had outdone himself this time; though he did say quite a lot of good things in the end. But as usual, it was a little too late.

And now with her gift in his hand, his comments seemed even more callous.

It had not been his intention to hurt her feelings. He simply wanted to help her because her work was good. He didn't have much experience in art but he had a good eye for talent.

So he just couldn't comprehend why someone as talented as Zoya would choose to sit quietly and do nothing about it. It was almost as if she were trying to hide herself in her little studio in some obscure corner of a park, with her little cat. What was his name? Ah yes, Zorba.

This made him wonder what name she had given him.

That is, if she even cared enough to name him. After all, he had spent just a few hours with her. He tried to rid his mind of her thoughts, and went back to the book. Though he had never read poetry before, the book, surprisingly, didn't bore him.

At first the lines didn't make much sense to Richard. The author, he thought, seemed to be speaking almost in a state of delirium. But as he went on, the lines alternated between an oddly comforting feel to an inexplicable liveliness.

*"This being human is a guest house. Every morning is a new arrival. A joy, a depression, a meanness, some momentary awareness comes as an unexpected visitor... Welcome and entertain them all. Treat each guest honorably. The dark thought, the shame, the malice, meet them at the door laughing, and invite them in. Be grateful for whoever comes, because each has been sent as a guide from beyond."*

*"Forget safety.*
*Live where you fear to live.*
*Destroy your reputation.*
*Be notorious."*

*"On a day*
*when the wind is perfect,*
*the sail just needs to open and the world is full of beauty.*
*Today is such a day."*

Eventually, he slipped into a deep sleep, his dreams a heady mix of balance sheets, dark eyes, couplets and curly hair.

# Bringing It to Life: Messages
# from Chapter Twelve – Transcending Fear

## *The Storyline*

Richard was confused by Zoya's insistence that she should not be pushed to expand her business or broaden her experiences. He suspected that it had to do with fear.

## *Messages*

*"Obstacles are what you see when you take your eyes off your goals."*

– Anonymous

## *Reflect on the following questions:*

- Do you fear the future?

- Do you allow obstacles to stop you from succeeding?

- Have you created a roadmap of where you want to go?

- Are you prepared to take the slow and steady approach to success, or are you looking for a quick fix?

- Do you confront fear or run from it?

- Do you analyze where your fear is coming from so you can overcome it at the root?

- Do you dare to walk the edge or always stay in your comfort zone?

- Do you manage your anxiety or let anxiety control you?

The fear of perceived obstacles is often a big roadblock on the path to success. Obstacles are part and parcel of life. The bigger your goals, the bigger your obstacles. Staying focused on your vision by having a clear road map and taking a slow and steady approach, allows you to not only overcome your challenges but also make breakthroughs.

Steve Jobs' approach to business and creativity went against convention, losing money along the way. Many people felt his ideas were too radical in the early days of his career, and they were not comfortable supporting his concepts because of that. Jobs recalled: "Of course it was impossible to connect the dots looking forward when I was in college. But it was very, very clear looking backwards, ten years later. Again, you can't connect the dots looking forward; you can only connect them looking backwards. So you have to trust that the dots will somehow connect in your future. You have to trust in something – your gut, destiny, life, karma, whatever. This approach has never let me down, and it has made all the difference in my life."

Jobs made Apple the most valuable company in the world, a feat he could never have achieved had he let the fear of change, difference and future get to him. Fear can limit your growth in every area of your life.

In certain situations, fear is appropriate. For example, if you are in front of a lion you will be fearful, which is totally normal. But fear that is reasonable is usually the exception, not the rule. Most of our fears are self-created and irrational.

Managing fear – and particularly being able to tell legitimate fear from the one that we have created in our minds – is a key attribute of any successful business person. When you start to let fear overtake you, you divert valuable energy from achieving the results you need.

Successful business people have always taken risks. No risk, no gain, as goes the saying. But this doesn't mean risk at any cost; it means taking calculated risk – risks you can define so you can understand and evaluate the worst thing that can happen. Calculating risks can help us manage our fear as well. When assessing a daunting problem, ask yourself: "If the worst happens, would I be able to live with it? If I can, then I might not have too much to fear." When you look at all the angles and minimize your risk, you may see that the upside is much higher. Or, if the worst comes to worst and you don't succeed in that particular opportunity, it won't be the end of the world.

We can find examples of the strength and power that managing our fear can give us in all sorts of situations. Azim went to Khorog in Tajikistan to work with an energy company. When he was due to leave, dense fog grounded the helicopter that took him back to the country's capital. The only option was to drive to Dushanbe, a challenging 12-hour journey through the Pamir mountain range, a rocky terrain where it isn't unusual to have to deal with flat tires. There are very few restaurants and restrooms along the way, but the mountains are spectacular and the skies thick with stars at night. Afghanistan, with all the chaos of war and poverty, lies across the Kofarnihon River.

At one point, the Tajik driver saw an eight-year-old girl selling apples in a bucket, but stopped by an elderly apple-seller's trolley. The eight-year-old stood smiling as if to ask innocently: "What's wrong with my apples?" The driver bought apples from the seller but eventually bought all the apples from the girl too. Why do you think he bought her apples? Was it her smile, or her heart-breaking innocence that persuaded him? The truth was that the little girl's forthrightness in her question nudged the driver's conscience.

So, if an eight-year-old girl in one of the poorest countries in the world can conquer her fears in order to achieve her goal, why can't we? You will not know your capacity to achieve until you push yourself to the edge.

A lot of people fear failure, which stops them from taking risks and achieving their full potential. The more you fear failure, the more you invite failure because wherever your attention goes and energy flows, that's what you attract in your life.

Marc Taylor, a psychologist for the US Navy, conducted a research on Olympic athletes to see what kind of performance-enhancing mental tactics they employed and how this affected their performance. Taylor found athletes who practiced visualizations and positive self-affirmations were better able to cope with the pressures of high-level competition, and were more likely to succeed.

There is an old story about a chief telling the children of a particular tribe that each of us has two wolves in our hearts, always fighting each other to control us – one good and the other evil. The children ask, "Which wolf will win?" The chief replies, "Whichever one you feed the most."

Which wolf are you feeding? The wolf of courage or the wolf of fear?

Once in a while you will fail and that's ok. It happens to all of us. When you decide to aim big, you start to feel insecure, create doubts and imagine obstacles on your path to success, but understand that failure is not permanent. People have lost loved ones, homes, health, jobs and yet rebuilt their lives. You can do the same with your business. Your competitor will always be better than you are in some areas of the business, and that's fine. Just ask yourself what value and outcome you are creating and how you can make a positive difference in your clients' lives. Focus on your past successes to create self-belief.

Finally, for some people, the fear is of success, not failure. They worry that they will not be able to handle it – that there will be pressure to live up to this success and they will lose their privacy. If you think you fear success, you have to ask yourself: do you want to stay in a cocoon all your life or realize your full potential?

Osho the mystic says: "A mother would never give birth to a child if she feared the pain of childbirth and a bird would never fly if it feared the unbounded skies."

*Challenge yourself with the following 'How to' exercises:*

1) CONFRONT fear rather than running away from it. Research has shown that repeated exposure lowers the psychological fear response until it is more manageable

or, in some cases, is gone completely. Start with small things like eating unfamiliar food or confronting a family member about a sensitive issue. If you tend to hold back at work, force yourself to come forward, perhaps by volunteering to take on new responsibility. Each time you face it, your fear will lose its sting.

2) WRITE down all your fears and analyze to see where they arise from. Is it something affecting your work, family, career or goals? Ask yourself: does my fear justify my potential failure to meet my goals? What do I need to do to address my fear and get beyond it? Understand that there are no failures. Every experience is either a success or a learning experience.

3) OVERCOME the fear of being wrong, fear of commitment or fear of disappointing others. Ask yourself the worst that could happen if you go wrong. Also, ask what will happen if you are right. Do you believe you can do it? Are you committed to execute? No commitment, no result. Trying to please others will get you nowhere. However, when you disappoint yourself, you disappoint all.

4) PRACTICE, PRACTICE, PRACTICE - most people fear speaking in public. If your fear is public speaking, practice giving talks in front of people whom you trust, who will encourage and bolster your confidence.

5) RE-ESTABLISH your trust in life. That way, life will give you whatever you need. When you lose trust, you also lose your connection with life.

6) LOOKING WITHIN helps you confront your fears as it requires you to re-evaluate your beliefs and codes that guide your decisions. When we sit still and turn our attention inward, we can find inner sources of energy, insight and courage. If you can clearly see your current predicament, you are primed to step beyond it. Meditation is a good technique for this end.

7) UNDERSTAND THE STRENGTH that comes from vulnerability. Being vulnerable also means you are more open to life. You have the capacity to observe, feel and learn more than someone who is closed or impassive.

   In business, cynicism and control breed fear. When you rid yourself of cynicism, you lose fear. The more you try to be in control, the less you are in control. The more you empower others, the more freedom you get. Don't try to be perfect because that is impossible. Excellence is good enough.

8) MANAGE STRESS, since stress and fear often come together. Stress is generally rooted in the fear of an imagined physical or emotional threat (e.g. not being able to meet a deadline). Exercise and meditation both have the power to lower stress levels and reduce negative feelings that could help you act more courageously in the face of challenges.

   What you are seeking *is* seeking you. Whatever is deep within you *is* being attracted to you. It may not come in the way you want it or *when* you want it. But when you trust this concept, you trust in yourself and you trust in life. Of course, you also have to do your part – have clear goals, focus, and work hard.

# Chapter Thirteen

# Honing the Art of Selling

*"Listen to people from your heart, as if your life depended on it, and you will find that in turn people will listen to you with all of theirs."*

– Chris Murray, *The Extremely Successful Salesman's Club*

Zoya was up by seven.

After a quick shower and an hour of meditation, she headed down the lane, ready to explore Istanbul. Janice had given her a small map with directions and also her cell phone number in case she got lost.

That morning, Zoya chose to wear a bottle-green sweater with her favorite pair of fitted blue jeans with a slim long brown overcoat and a chocolate brown woolen scarf. A pair of brown suede boots completed her attire. She wore her favorite pearl drop earrings and left her hair loose, enjoying the morning breeze.

The sun was just beginning to rise and the entire road was suffused with a warm golden-pink hue. The air was quite cool and she grabbed the lapels of her coat closer. There were curio shops lined up on both sides of the street and a few shopkeepers sat outside, trying to tempt her in. Sensing that she was Indian, some even sang old Hindi songs. Seemingly, Raj Kapoor was still quite the rage in this part of the world.

As she neared the edge of the public garden that joined the Blue Mosque and Hagia Sophia, a flurry of travel guides surrounded her, offering to show her the sights at cheap prices. She glanced at her watch. It was only nine. She wasn't sure if the Mosque would be open for tourists.

Just then one of the guides, a slender, wiry man with a warm smile and a Johnny Depp hairdo, came forward. "It's good that you are early. There won't be much of a crowd now," he said as he gestured towards the Blue Mosque.

She decided Johnny Depp it was; pleasant yet quirky. Good combination. She asked, "How much?"

"Anything you wish!" he said laughing. He had a nice easy laugh and deep brown eyes.

Seeing the deal done, the others walked away, grumbling a little to themselves. The guide introduced himself as Baran and said he had been working as a guide now for almost 13 years. They entered the mosque from the right side of the building. It was customary to cover one's head and remove one's shoes. Luckily, Zoya was wearing a scarf, so she didn't have to look for one. She wrapped her boots in the plastic bags provided near the entrance and entered the courtyard lining the mosque.

Baran maintained a constant stream of words, regaling her with stories of how the Mosque was built, peppering the tale with anecdotes and incidents, many of which seemed like exaggerations. But his animated stories brought life to the mosque, which was built by the then monarch, Sultan Ahmet, to rival the grandeur of the nearby Hagia Sofia.

The cool blue visage of the mosque, with its voluptuous cascade of domes reined in by six slender minarets, did form an incredible façade.

When they walked into the Mosque, she was immediately seized by its beauty and the intricate work on the walls. The interiors were lined with İznik tiles with beautiful blue tulip motifs, while the marble pulpit featured a mother-of-pearl relief and the entire structure was interspersed at regular intervals with 260 stained-glass windows. The light filtered through the colored glass to infuse the air with a surreal, incandescent hue, while the huge glass chandeliers hanging from the tall domed ceiling added to the dreamlike effect.

Baran told her that the interior was intended to be a replica of paradise. She sat there for a long time, taking in its beauty and enjoying the silence. Even Baran retreated to a quiet corner, letting her be. He seemed to know when to create stories and when to let the stories do the talking.

Zoya was seized by an urge to call Richard and share this moment with him. It was a feeling that she couldn't describe at that moment.

He would have liked this place. And she had a feeling that they would enjoy discussing the architecture, debating over which sections were more appealing. And not only the architecture, they could talk easily on almost anything. In fact they had started off on a great note. They had had a good time discussing plenty. *You mean the part where you talked and he listened?* the tiny voice inside her asked wryly.

Firmly shrugging off the voice, Zoya got back to her earlier happy thoughts. Everything had been so good, so good… until Bobby had surfaced. At times, she felt Bobby existed solely to vex her. He would suddenly appear at the most inopportune of moments, unneeded and unwarranted. In fact, even after she had left her first job, she would run into him intermittently at galleries and art exhibitions.

On second thought, he was always present whenever there was some big change awaiting her. He would be there on the horizon, shouting hoarsely to get her attention on things she didn't want to deal with on her own.

She shuddered to think what change he was heralding now. Just then, she saw Baran gesturing to her about the time. Oh yes, it was time to go now. It was already eleven and she still had a lot of Istanbul to cover.

They came out and headed towards the tomb of Ahmed I, the Sultan who created the Blue Mosque. She learnt that the Blue Mosque had been created chiefly to reassert Ottoman power and was built on the site of the former palace of the Byzantine emperors next to the hippodrome, and facing Hagia Sophia.

Sadly, the Sultan had died when he was a young man of 27, just a year after the completion of his masterpiece. He was then buried outside the mosque next to his wife and three sons.

They stood quietly before the unadorned tombs of the Sultan and his family.

"So this is what it all finally boils down to," Zoya murmured.

"Yes, but look at the magnificent legacy he created. It lives on long after he is gone," Baran added.

"But he was so young! Just 27!"

"Madam it's not how long we live, but what we have created during that life. What have we left to the world? Is it a little more beautiful, a little more thoughtful, and a little kinder because of us? It is what will stay on regardless of whether you die at 27 or 80."

"Wow Baran! You said it beautifully," Zoya said with a smile.

"Beauty inspires beauty, madam," he said with a bow.

"You know just what to say, don't you?" she laughed.

She thanked Baran with a generous fee and bid adieu to the Blue Mosque. She came out to see the sun now high in the sky and headed towards a nearby restaurant. It was a small, cozy café with outdoor seating. The owners had lined up space heaters at regular intervals to beat the December chill.

The menu was detailed and everything looked quite interesting. She finally opted for *ezme, a* spicy tomato and pepper salad, and *patlican dolma*, a delicious spread of stuffed dried eggplants.

She washed it all down with a cup of hot Turkish coffee, a bittersweet beverage that suffused her body with warmth. It felt glorious to be alive and she stretched out her arms, enjoying the afternoon sun on her skin.

★

The rest of the day passed in a flurry of activity.

After a quick tour of Hagia Sophia, a visit to the Cistern Basilica and a rapid shopping trip in the Grand Bazaar, Zoya decided to end the day with a quiet stroll in Yildiz Park in Besiktas.

By late afternoon, the weather had started to change. The sky was steadily gathering a smattering of clouds. Soon brief snatches of sunlight were followed by intermittent dark clouds and a gentle breeze blew.

Zoya hurried back towards the garden entrance as the first rain-drops began to splatter. The drizzle quickly turned into a steady downpour. She hurried to get under one of the large oak trees and hoped her coat would not get too wet. It was the only one she had brought.

Fortunately, the sun came out again after ten minutes. She gingerly headed towards a park bench, shivering a little, wanting to salvage her money from her coat pocket and hoping that it had not soaked through.

Not much water had collected on the bench so she was able to brush it off with her hand and sit. She quickly removed the dampened notes from her coat pocket, waving them gently in the breeze to dry them. While she flapped the notes, she decided to remove her boots as well and allow them to dry.

Just as she bent down to remove them, she noticed a small black beetle trapped in a puddle of water under the bench. It kept trying to wiggle out, but failed at each attempt. A rivulet of water was rapidly advancing towards the puddle from up the slope and would soon engulf it, and wash the beetle away.

Zoya searched for a twig to help the insect, but there was nothing around. She quickly rummaged through her pockets and her fingers brushed against her room keys. She angled the pointy end of the key towards the beetle, hoping to coax it out. But it refused to climb on to the key. The cold, shiny end of the key was obviously unfamiliar.

It would drift towards the key, hesitate and then pull back, struggling weakly against the current. It seemed to trust the familiar puddle, even if it meant dying a slow death. Zoya finally hoisted the beetle out with the broad flat end of the key and deposited it on the bark of an oak tree close by.

A glance at her watch told her it was time to head back to her hotel. She had an early morning flight to Konya and her shopping spree at the Grand Bazaar meant her suitcase had to be rearranged.

Suddenly, she was tempted to call Richard again and check how his sales conference was going. It would have been over by now. But she quickly reasoned that knowing him, he would be extremely busy.

Their argument came flooding back to her: his remarks, comments, everything.

Zoya could shrug off most comments but he had called her *scared*. But if she really believed he was wrong, then why did it bother her so much? Yes, why couldn't she let it go? Could it be that she was upset because he had said it, or because in some tiny corner of her heart she thought he might be right?

And then it slowly dawned on her: *Maybe Zoya Rahman was scared of coming out of her puddle.*

She had probably become too comfortable in her own little world, her everyday rituals, almost withdrawing from life. Probably her mind was now using the excuse of going within, not to know herself better, but to escape the unfamiliar and the unknown and cling to false expressions of security.

"The ways of the ego are subtle indeed." She smiled at herself, thinking of Richard's words, and murmured a silent *thank you* to him.

She checked her watch. It was already six o'clock. He must be getting ready for his board meeting. It wouldn't be right to disturb him now, even if it was to thank him.

She finally decided to give him a call the next day, just before she flew to Konya.

She was feeling relieved now as she sauntered back to her B&B, excited about the next day.

## Bringing It to Life: Messages from Chapter Thirteen – Honing the Art of Selling

### *The Storyline*

Zoya learns that choosing a guide to Istanbul's famous Blue Mosque is all about finding someone who appeals to her particular needs and sensibilities. Baran the tour guide is charming, knows his subject, understands what Zoya is looking for and is able to make her experience enjoyable. He has the art of selling.

### *Messages*

*"I will greet this day with love in my heart."*

– Og Mandino

### *Reflect on the following questions:*

- Do you know your customer? If not, what do you need to do to know your customer well?

- What do you need to do to create a memorable buying experience for your customer?

- Have you identified your unique selling strength?

- How do you continuously improve your selling?

- What do you do to ensure that you are authentic when selling your products and services?

- Do you genuinely care about your customer?

- Have you mastered your emotions?

- Do you persist till you succeed?

- Do you engage in frequent face-to-face meetings with your clients?

Do you get demotivated by every 'no' you receive or are actually motivated by it because it gets you closer to a 'yes'? Facts *tell* but emotions *sell*, and most sales happen through emotion. Sometimes you just like a person and want to do business with him. The key is to learn how to touch the emotional chord that will compel people to purchase what you sell.

We are all selling every day at home or at work. We sell to our spouse or our children when we discuss our viewpoint, outlook or holiday plans. It is important to care about your prospects, whether they are in your work life or your home. You must be very interested in the prospect's needs and have a genuine desire to make a difference. Such honesty builds credibility and trust, because the person realizes that you are keeping their best interests at heart. The key is to understand their perspective to fulfil their needs and accommodate their interests as well.

When Brian was younger and struggling, he took on a sales job because he had no other options. He started work early in the morning and would work until late at night, running from prospect to prospect. Even after a long day of hard work, his results were dismal. At the same time, another person in his office came in late, had time for coffee, went out for lunch and left early but sold far more than any other person in the company. Brian asked his teammate to show him his sales presentation and his colleague was kind enough to do so. He learned that his colleague's sales presentation far enhanced what he called his "blah, blah, blah" presentation. Eager to improve, Brian began reading books about selling, listening to audio programs and attending seminars. He became a sales guru, and has been teaching the art of selling for the past 30 years. What drove him, and can drive you too, was genuine interest, the desire to learn, grow and get better at the job every day. Here are Brian's 7 steps to the sales cycle:

1.  Prospecting: If you don't have people to sell to, you really have nothing to sell. Everything starts with prospecting, which is essentially the process in which you separate suspects from prospects.

2.  Building Rapport: If people like you, they will find a way to do business with you. If people don't like you, they will find a reason not to buy from you.

3.  Identifying Needs: Funny thing about sales: they are only made to people who have a want or a need that your product or service can fill or solve.

4.  Delivering Persuasive Presentations: You need to be able to effectively present your ideas/solutions/ company in a manner that is persuasive, professional and targeted. No matter what form your presentation takes, being prepared and having clear objectives are two most important aspects of an effective presentation.

5.  Overcoming Objections: Around 99 percent of your sales cycle will be filled with customer objections.

If you can learn to not only expect objections but to anticipate and plan for them, they will lose the sting they once had.

6.  Closing the Sale: While most non-sales professionals think that closing or making a sale is the only thing that sales professional do, it is in fact just one step to what is often a very long sales cycle. While it may be the most important step, successful closes come after completing each of the previous steps and not by jumping directly to the sales' hunt.

7.  Getting Repeat Sales and Referrals: The final stage in the sales cycle is really the first step to your next sales cycle. Asking for referrals from your customers is, for some reason, something that most sales professionals do not do. While there are many excuses that people give to explain why they don't ask for referrals, there are no good reasons for not doing so.

A question we are often asked is: how can you be genuine and attend to your customer's needs when you have strict sales targets to meet? The issue is short-term versus long-term success. Long-term success starts with trust, with building a relationship. If you are trying to make a quick sale but damage your customer's trust, you may make your numbers in the short term, but it will be very hard to regain your credibility and get repeat business. Therefore, balancing your need to meet short-term targets and at the same time build long-term relationship and trust will create the optimum outcome.

*Challenge yourself with the following 'How to' exercise:*

1) CARE about the customer, not just your product. Realize that no sale will happen unless the customer takes interest. The customer will only take interest when you understand his or her problem and know how your product caters to their needs.

2) Prioritize them – your client, customer, family member – and their needs, wants and wishes. Find practical ways to help them with their problems. Let them know that it is about them.

3) LISTEN with your eyes and your heart, with undivided attention and without judgment. Appeal to buyers' emotions because that's what excites them more than facts.

4) THINK BIG – if you have a big target then your ideas and outlook will change to support that. Ask what success looks like to you.

5) MASTER your emotions. Don't take rejection personally because it's not about you, it's about the client. Rejection merely means your product does not match their needs; they can't afford it or they're interested in something different. You have to remember that you cannot win every sale. Nobody does. You cannot be good for everyone, and this does not reflect your worth as a person. You are unique and your services will appeal to some but not everyone. The baseball team that wins the world championship could lose about one-third of their games.

6) PERSIST in your selling; don't give up easily. Make

one more call, one more knock, one more presentation. Some people stop just before they achieve their goal.

7)  BELIEVE in your product and services and use them yourself so you can explain them better. Your conviction in the goodness of your product will show up in your demeanor. Enhance word-of-mouth selling by giving extraordinary value.

8)  HAVE face-to-face meetings because they lead to more sales and help build rapport and great relationships.

9)  READ or listen to sales books to learn how to become better. *The Greatest Salesman in the World* by Og Mandino and Brian Tracy's *The Psychology of Selling* are two good examples.

10)  ASK the great questions: "why", "what" and "how". Also, show that you are inclined to "listen" – a key skill that will increase your relationship with your client.

If you are afraid of rejection, you will make very little in sales. See rejection as an opportunity to learn from your mistakes, and significantly improve the product and service. See every 'no' as one step forward towards getting a 'yes'. Remember that a rejection is nothing personal; the prospect is just not the right fit. Maybe a bigger sale is around the corner.

# Chapter Fourteen

# Creating Abundance through Giving

*"You give but little when you give of your possessions.
It is when you give of yourself that you truly give."*

— Khalil Gibran, *The Prophet*

Richard woke up with a start. It was already 6.30 in the morning. He rushed to the bathroom after ordering a quick breakfast through room service. At his request, the company had booked him at a hotel closer to the airport. He had deliberately opted to stay away from the Grand Hyatt, which was the conference venue, choosing to drive to the location when required. This allowed him the peace and quiet to complete his work without the hassle of mindless socializing.

He went down 30 minutes later with a croissant in his hand, and found his car already waiting to take him to the Grand Hyatt.

It was a short, swift ride and before he knew it, the driver was already parking the car near the hotel entrance.

He was greeted by his executive assistant, Peter Simpson, as soon as he entered the lobby. Peter quickly briefed him on the event specifics and led him to the banquet area. There was still an hour before the event would begin but Richard liked to arrive early to double-check everything.

After going through the talking points and checking the list of the channel partners attending the conference, he excused himself for some quiet time.

He quickly repeated in his mind the key messages he needed to reiterate; the important places where he needed to lay emphasis, people he needed to meet in person, and finally the deliverables he expected to take back by the end of the day.

There was a lot riding on how the conference went. If he could garner the support of major dealers on the forecasted numbers, it would bode well for his meeting with the board in the evening.

The conference began well, but soon it was evident that the dealers were not ready to jump on the bandwagon just yet. There was a lot of counter questioning and back and forth on the numbers. Most of them were too concerned about the market and were not willing to take the risk.

In the end, Richard had to trim the forecast a bit to enable the group to reach a consensus. After the meeting, he held extended one-on-one meetings with the key dealers over coffee.

After long, drawn-out discussions and a few successes, the dealers soon retired to their rooms to get ready for evening cocktails. Though his hotel was a short distance away, Richard opted to stick around at the Grand Hyatt for the cocktail party and the board meetings since both events were being held at the same hotel.

He dismissed his executive assistant and took a lazy stroll in the hotel's garden to clear his mind, enjoying the chilly winter breeze. He had always enjoyed winters and looked forward to spending time outdoors.

After about 20 minutes, he walked towards the men's room to freshen up for the party. The room was empty and he was able to quickly change into fresh clothes. He was just buttoning his coat, when someone lumbered into the washroom. He turned back to give a polite nod to the stranger when he noticed it wasn't a stranger.

It was Mr. Goodman, the board member who had been negative about some of Richard's business proposals. As usual, he didn't seem in a particular hurry to acknowledge him, shuffling uncomfortably and trying not to make eye contact.

But this time Richard was determined to not let him get away. It was then that he noticed the stain. It was a long, dull, red stain that had spread right across the center of Goodman's chest to his rather large paunch.

For a moment, he was almost tempted to laugh, but the old man's obvious discomfort quickly dampened his amusement.

It was evident that there had been a wine mishap. The old man frantically started washing away the stain, but the water only seemed to exacerbate the problem.

Richard checked his watch. The cocktail party must have already begun and the board meeting would start in another 20 minutes.

His first instinct was to leave the man alone. It was fairly evident that Mr. Goodman didn't like him. And to be caught in this situation, maybe Richard's presence was embarrassing him even more. Also, his assistant Peter had already messaged twice.

But one more look at Goodman, and he suddenly wondered how Zoya would have reacted. Knowing her, she would have stayed back to help, even if the person in front of her didn't want any.

"Maybe you should take off the shirt and try to wash it off," Richard ventured.

The man simply grunted in response, but proceeded to unbutton his shirt. His hands were fumbling and he seemed to be growing more nervous with every passing minute.

Richard deliberated whether they should call room service to take care of it, but that would have drawn unnecessary attention and wasted more time. He quickly helped Mr. Goodman unbutton his shirt. He squeezed out a little soap from the dispenser and rubbed the stain, while Mr. Goodman stood quietly in his undershirt, looking both embarrassed and grateful. But in spite of his best efforts, the stain did not budge much. It simply changed from dark red to a dull brown.

"Do you have another shirt? I don't think this stain is going to come off."

"Er… no. I'm flying back after the meeting and have already checked in my luggage."

They both stood there wondering what to do. Richard's shirt would never fit him, especially around the middle. "The gift shop!" Richard suddenly remembered.

"Pardon me?" asked Goodman.

"The hotel gift shop! I'm sure we will find something there. Here, wear your shirt."

Richard helped Goodman to swiftly button his shirt and led him outside. The hotel gift shop was on the other side of the lobby and they both walked quickly to avoid running into anyone they knew. Though it wouldn't have been a big deal, Richard knew that the other board members would have sniggered over this incident for a long time afterwards.

The gift shop had mostly artifacts and souvenirs and very few items of clothing, especially for men. And irrespective of what shirt one selected, getting the right fit was a problem.

The store's clerk pranced about worriedly, trying to suggest an alternative. After a lot of searching, they finally spotted a pale lemon yellow shirt.

Luckily, the gift shop had a trial room and they were spared the long walk back to the washroom.

Mr. Goodman, meanwhile, shambled out of the fitting room, the buttons of his new shirt stretching a little too snugly over his stomach. He stood there like an unsure schoolboy, waiting for Richard's feedback. It was obvious that someone else did his shopping for him, most probably his wife.

"I think it looks just fine."

It had to look fine. The shirt seemed a little too tight, but there was no other option. Richard suddenly remembered the blue tie he was wearing in the morning. That would go well with the shirt and maybe even cover up any gaps.

Ten frenetic minutes later, Mr. Goodman was good to go. Richard and the clerk stood there, happily admiring their handiwork, while Mr. Goodman smiled shyly.

"So, I'll take your leave now, sir. I have to get to the cocktail party. I'll see you later at the meeting."

"Richard!"

He looked back to see Mr. Goodman with a faint smile spreading over his face.

"Thank you," he mumbled.

Richard nodded back with a smile and after a pause, rushed towards the pool for the evening party. He was already late but he didn't seem to care very much now.

# Bringing It to Life: Messages from Chapter Fourteen – Creating Abundance through Giving

### The Storyline

Despite running late, Richard helps Mr. Goodman solve an embarrassing problem. To do so, he had to forget his past experience with Mr. Goodman and see him simply as a fellow human being with a problem. By giving his time and showing real concern without any thought of personal gain, he helped Mr. Goodman save face, and in doing, so gained the elderly man's respect.

### Messages

*"To find yourself, lose yourself in the service of others."*

– Mahatma Gandhi

### Reflect on the following questions:

- Do you give unconditionally? Think of a good thought for someone. How do you feel?

- Do you have a "tight-fist" mentality, one that neither gives nor receives?

- When you pass on, what will you take with you?

- Do you have something to give – time, knowledge, experience, money?

- Do you give with respect, humility and love?

- Do you wait for the perfect time to give?

- Do you give the benefit of doubt to someone before judging him?

- Do you find an excuse not to give, or instead find an excuse to give?

- Do you keep a score of how much you've given to someone?

Do you strive to give up anger, resentment, jealousy and negative ego? Giving is a potent force and it works in all walks of life. When you give your customers extraordinary value, they give you more business. When you give to your colleagues, there is more harmony and camaraderie. If you mentor your subordinates, they perform better. When you are a loving spouse, you create harmony. If you love your children, they feel more secure. If your business gives to society, you earn credibility.

A study by the Reputation Institute suggests that Microsoft, the Walt Disney Company, Google, BMW and Daimler are viewed as the most responsible corporations, with marks based on three criteria: citizenship, governance and workplace.

Disney took high marks (49.6 percent of those surveyed gave it thumbs up) due to its environmental programs like carbon offset goals. BMW's commitment to transparency, and defending and protecting whistleblowers, earned it high marks from 48.8

percent of those surveyed; while Google received high marks from 51.1 percent of those surveyed because of its famously positive working environment.

Whether as an individual, family member or businessperson, make "giving" a part of your life, and experience the power it creates.

In their book, *Why Good Things Happen to Good People*, Dr. Stephen Post and journalist Jill Neimark show how giving unlocks the doors to health, happiness and a longer life. They include a 50-year study showing that people who give during their high school years have better physical and mental health throughout their lives. Other studies show that older people who give, live longer than those who don't. Helping others has been shown to bring health benefits to those with chronic illness, including HIV, multiple sclerosis and heart problems. Studies also show that people of all ages who help others on a regular basis, even in small ways, feel happiest.

Consider this story by an anonymous author: Two brothers inherited their father's land. They divided the land in half and each one farmed his own section. In course of time, the older brother married and had six children, while the younger brother never married. One night, the younger brother lay awake thinking that his brother needed more land to farm because he had six children to feed, while he was childless.

So that night, the younger brother gathered a large bundle of wheat from his side of the land and climbed the hill that separated the two farms, leaving the wheat on his brother's land.

Earlier that same night, the older brother also lay awake, thinking that in his old age his wife and children will take care of him, while his brother would always be alone. So that night, he too dropped a large bundle of wheat on his younger brother's land.

The next morning, both brothers were surprised to see the amount of grain in their respective barns unchanged. This continued for a few nights until the two brothers realized what was happening, and embraced in joy.

We can always find something to give. The joy of giving does not spring from the availability of dispensable resources. True richness is defined not in how much you *have* but how much you can *give*! Meaning, fulfillment and happiness come from making a difference and giving happiness to others.

## Challenge yourself with the following 'How to' exercises:

1)  SHARE a compliment, loving thought, smile, blessing, positive feedback, a prayer, forgiveness, gratitude, insight, an idea or money.

2)  PRACTICE giving the benefit of doubt to someone when you are tempted to judge them. Do this by giving the best possible interpretation to the situation. For example, when you feel someone has bad-mouthed you, ask what could be the best possible interpretation of this. Could you be mistaken? Could it be that the person who informed you of the bad-mouthing is trying to cause a friction between you and the person in question? There are many possibilities. The outcome of this approach is that you will feel more at peace.

3) Give UNCONDITIONALLY; don't expect anything in return, just like Nature shares its riches (the shining sun, the scent of a flower) with us, with open arms.

4) DON'T keep a score of when, why and how you give. As the theologian and author William Barkley has said: "Always give without remembering and receive without forgetting."

5) THANK people who asked you to help them because they gave you the opportunity to give; it's a pleasure to help.

7) GIVE UP on negative traits – jealousy (someone's gain is not your loss; the universe is abundant); ego (by realizing that you need others to help you); anger (it's no one's fault; it's your choice to be angry); and negativity (look at the best interpretation, be grateful for what you have, check on your negative thoughts).

8) KNOW that you can choose your reactions to situations, and that you can choose reactions that bring you peace. Ask yourself: if jealousy or anger or negativity do not bring me peace, then why choose these reactions? You have a choice. It's not easy to do, but try to lower your frustration and anger levels, and prevent them from consuming you.

9) GO THE EXTRA MILE with your customer – give more than you're paid for, and you'll increase your value in your customer's eyes.

10) START your day by giving to your family. What can you give? Time, knowledge, attention, resources, a smile, a patient ear, forgiveness, a non-judgmental

attitude, a prayer, a hug or a compliment. Continue the trend at your workplace by giving to your customers, colleagues and other stakeholders.

# Chapter Fifteen

# Living and Working in Zest

*"Zest is the secret of all beauty. There is no beauty that is attractive without zest."*

– Christian Dior

It was nearly 11.30 at night when Richard finally exited the board meeting. He knew he would always remember this walk, this night. It would be indelibly imprinted on his mind. He was conscious of each step he took, the ruckus of the cicadas singing in the adjacent garden, the numbing chill of the December night, and the rich taste of the luscious *Künefe* dessert still lingering on his tongue. It was as if everything were passing in slow motion.

The enormity of his decision was now beginning to dawn on him. There would have to be a lot of changes. His pay would probably go down, along with the perks that came with it. He would have to look for a new place in San Jose; probably, even sell his apartment in Manhattan. There would be a lot of speculation in the market about his decision. His peers would probably even doubt its soundness. But all of this could still not quell the spring in his step. He would be back to the design board where he belonged, where it all began. And with his travel schedule petering out, he would have so much more time for his other pursuits. Maybe he could even start lecturing at the university again. Maybe even coach William in soccer!

A good long discussion with the board had slowly uncovered their real concerns about the new investment. They just weren't confident about the technology. The R&D team was young and eager to go, but they were still inexperienced. And in the current market situation, it was difficult to find someone senior to lead the development. A lot of money had already been wasted on trials and the ongoing slowdown was not helping the bottom line. It was just too risky to invest in such a scenario.

It was then that it dawned on Richard that he had done it before and he could do it again. Design was in his very DNA. Of course that would mean stepping down from his current position, but on the upside, he could start creating something, building something all over again.

The board had initially been shocked by his proposal and had quashed it. But finally, a gentle nudge from the usually reticent Mr. Goodman stoked the discussion again. In the end, they had unanimously agreed to give him one year to bring about the required breakthrough in the technology.

Life was coming around in full circle. It did look scary, but there was a sign of a new beginning.

He was about to walk past the gift shop, when he remembered something. He headed towards the music section and selected a miniature version of the Ud, a Turkish musical instrument very similar to the guitar but with a soulful, poignant twang. It was for William. The boy was already learning to play the guitar and was always very curious about music.

As he was leaving the shop, he spotted a bracelet, its silver charms glinting in the glare of the yellow store light. It was crafted with bright blue stones; the same shade of blue that Zoya had worn. He lifted the bracelet out from its stand and examined it. The stones felt smooth and cool in his fingers and the silver charms tinkled softly.

"This bracelet is made of original Turkish turquoise and set in silver," the shopkeeper told him. "Turquoise is considered to be a talisman of luck, success, ambition and creativity and the wearer…"

"That's great. I'll take it!" Richard smiled as he cut him short and handed over his credit card.

## Bringing It to Life: Messages from Chapter Fifteen – Zestfully Living and Working

### *The Storyline*

For the first time in many years, Richard felt a spring in his step because he had decided to do what he loved, rather than what he felt he had to do.

### *Messages*

*"Nothing else matters much; not wealth, nor learning, nor even health... without this gift: the spiritual capacity to keep zest in living. This is the creed of creeds, the final deposit and distillation of all important faiths: that you should be able to believe in life."*

– Harry Emerson Fosdick

### *Reflect on the following questions:*

- Do you see every opportunity as full of zest?

- How often do you exercise your choice to be zestful?

- Do you examine what bothers you and why?

- Do you eliminate those things from your life that drain your energy?

- Do you find some joy in everything you do – even in mundane tasks?

- Do you, in the midst of difficulty, reflect on or create an inspiring goal and focus on it?

- Do you begin your day with gratitude, thinking of five things you are grateful for?

- Do you exercise regularly, thereby increasing the feel-good hormones in your body?

- Do you consciously aim to create an inspiring and uplifting environment at home and work?

Zest creates joy; it gives you the ability to appreciate life during both ups and downs; the drive to face challenges in a positive manner. Zest comes from and is fuelled by what excites you, makes you enthusiastic and passionate. If you know what this is, do more of it. Maybe you don't have too many opportunities at your workplace to do all the things you love but if you can identify what you really enjoy, you get greater zest.

When you are not excited about your work, it infiltrates your personal life. But when you are living and working with passion – with zest – you are happier and others will find it a pleasure to be around you. When you do the right thing, deep joy is imminent. When you are living and working with passion, it is contagious and inspires others. Work and life are then less stressful.

Many of us believe that zest won't fit into our busy lives – that that kind of thing is for someone more resourceful, or with a less complicated life and fewer responsibilities. We may think that it's easy to talk about having a zest for life if you were born with a silver spoon. But zest isn't about money or privilege. Zest is about feeling passion in your own life, rather than waiting for 'someday' when things change enough for you to feel excited about your life and work.

Sustaining zest in our lives can be a challenge, and the troubles and various commitments in our lives can make us wonder if zest has any place in it. Anyone with financial constraints, personal lows like an unsuccessful relationship, health issues, and aging parents would know that these challenges can make zest almost unattainable.

But when you respond in a positive way, you can still generate that spark. So don't make excuses; feel that you deserve it. After all, history is full of examples of people who have gone through immense suffering and still found a zest for life. Nelson Mandela and Victor Frankl were examples we used earlier in the book.

So how do we get more zest into our lives? At home, we all have things that excite us – maybe not doing the laundry or taking out the garbage, but spending uninterrupted time with loved ones or eating together or spending time on a hobby. Whatever fills you with joy, do it. The more you do of it, the more zest you create in your life.

Finding things that excite you about life helps increase your zest – but doing the right thing does too. How you build your relationships with loved ones can have an impact on how zestful you are. If you have loving and jovial relationships, you enhance your energy.

If you have a zest for life, you produce more and are more attuned to your customers' needs, who in turn enjoy spending time with you. Your work isn't simply a means to make a living; it becomes a place of excitement, enthusiasm and positive outcomes.

Most of us get bored with menial tasks, but reframing the task and being fully in the present moment, helps. When Azim goes to large social functions, he doesn't have much zest because making small talk with so many people drains him. To overcome that and improve his zest in these situations, he focuses on just two or three people and really engages with them. Being a good listener and finding out about their work gets Azim excited. So finding ways to make apparently menial tasks exciting is how you create zest in life.

You may not have experienced zest but you can see it in other people – the spring in their step, their enthusiasm, energy, pride and passion. To some people, zest may feel overrated, just a show that people put on to tell the outside world that they are happy. But real zest can't be fabricated. Real zest comes from within and is thus contagious and admirable and gives you the drive to get more done in less time and do it with gusto.

People who practice zest embrace life as an adventure and push the envelope. They see possibility where others only see problems. They do big things and bring other people along on their journey. Zest is transformative because it's not a fixed trait, but a mindset. By cultivating it, we can all experience a life of energy and enthusiasm, which improves our effectiveness dramatically, especially at the workplace.

Try to create a workplace that not only displays your own zest, but helps cultivate it in your employees. Praise people at every opportunity; make sure that your team has access to your positive mentorship and coaching; and encourage meritocracy, not mediocrity or politics. Set up an uplifting décor in your office, one that is vibrant. Ensure clarity of goals and roles. A zestful workplace is a happier workplace, and in the end, a more profitable workplace.

In a survey that was carried out on more than 9,800 full-time employees, Christopher Peterson, a psychology professor at the University of Michigan, and his colleagues found that personal zest was positively connected to an employee's level of work satisfaction, overall life satisfaction, and belief that his work was a calling, rather than just a job.

Zestful employees result in lower absenteeism, lower turnover and higher group morale, leading to a better bottom line.

### Challenge yourself with the following 'How to' exercises:

1) RECALL the last time you felt amazing, full of love, joy and experienced a zest for life. What were you doing? Replicate that activity.

2) WRITE down what bothers you, upsets you, drains you of energy and really examine why. Develop a plan to do less of those things.

3) JOY is contagious. It has a force of energy that fills people with optimism. Do something that makes you happy. Does listening to music make you happy? Or enjoying a quiet cup of coffee, or golfing? Regularly do the things that you enjoy to invite more joy in your life.

4) DO something that has long-term value for you, not just instant gratification. Some practical examples are exercising, reading good literature or engaging in financial planning.

5) FIND pleasure in everything you do, even routine tasks. Become engrossed in small things like household chores; make it an art. Be the very best you can be at that.

6) DELEGATE things that don't excite you.

7) ASK your boss for things to do that are good for the company and that you are good at. Show how it can benefit the company in terms of increased sales and better team work. Assist your boss with his or her goals. Show how the work that you're good at, positively impacts the bottom line.

8) READ your inspiring goal in the midst of difficulty. When Azim was working as a volunteer with Afghan refugees, he saw many small children, who had lost their parents, begging in the streets. It was heart-breaking. As he entered a rug shop he saw a powerful quote on a small rug pinned on the wall: "Obstacles are what you see when you take your eyes off your goals" (we shared this quote at the Messages from Chapter Twelve).

9) START your day by thinking of five things you're grateful for. This gives you a positive start.

10) EXERCISE regularly.

11) CREATE an inspiring and uplifting environment at home and work, and live a life of integrity and principle.

You are the master of your destiny. If you wait for someone else to create zest in your life, it may never happen or you may end up waiting a very long time. However, if you decide that you are in charge of how you feel, then you have the capacity to turn things around now!

# Chapter Sixteen

# Discovering the Liberty
# of Detachment

*"The Sufi is One who does not care when something is taken from him, but who does not cease to seek for what he has not."*

— Idries Shah, *Aprendera Aprender*

Richard looked around for a quiet corner and picked a chair right down the hall. He headed down the corridor slowly; in fact he was in no hurry to get to it. But finally that frontier too was crossed. Now there was nothing else to do, except call.

He looked at the phone and the number on the post-it, its bright yellow color taunting him, teasing him a little.

He tried to frame his words but nothing came to mind. He gulped a couple of times. His throat felt parched. He decided to drink some water. But that would mean a long walk back to the food court.

He stretched himself, trying to flex his tired shoulders and suddenly felt the hard edge of the book press into his chest. He removed it and picked out a page randomly.

*"Put your thoughts to sleep,*
*do not let them cast a shadow*
*over the moon of your heart.*
*Let go of thinking."*

The stanza quietly, stoically, beckoned him. He decided to let go and dialed the number. The phone at the other end rang four times before it was answered. A cool, unruffled voice took in the details. He was again put on hold. He had a sudden urge to end the call and put it all behind him, but the book in his hand calmed him. Finally, someone answered the call.

"Hello," a wavering voice answered.

"Hi Dad, it's Richard!" There was a long silence at the other end. Maybe he had disconnected the call.

"Hello! Are you there?" Richard asked hesitantly.

"Yes, I'm here," the voice seemed steadier now.

"Hi Dad, I've been meaning to call." Meaning to call, after 16 years! God, it sounded ridiculous even to his own ears. "I was planning to come to Houston next month. It's William's birthday on the 10th. Thought I'd catch up with you as well." *He wasn't making any sense. Dad was in San Antonio.*

"I mean, I'll come to San Antonio first and then take a flight to LA."

"That would be nice," his father's voice softened.

Emboldened by the reply, he decided to venture further. "Uh, Dad, another thing – I was wondering if you would like to accompany me to LA. The Eagles are performing and I was planning on taking William for their next concert."

"The Eagles! Are they still on?" his tone had suddenly acquired a more enthusiastic timbre.

"Yes, they are!" Richard replied.

"God, I thought they had retired a long time back!" his father said, laughing a little. But then as suddenly, his voice quickly changed back to its former gruff tone. "Uh, I guess I'll have to check."

"I thought it would be a good opportunity for you, me and William to spend some time together. Let me know," Richard persisted gently.

"Uh well, okay then. Sounds good to me," he agreed, albeit hesitantly.

"Ok. I'll call you next week to plan it." There was silence at the other end. Nobody spoke for a few seconds. Richard was about to hang up, when his father suddenly said, "Thanks. I'll wait for your call."

Richard hung up, tears welling up in his eyes. But they were a different kind of tears. They brought with them an overwhelming sense of joy. That's when he realized joy happens when you fit in with your life, when you fit in so harmoniously that whatever you are doing becomes your joy.

And each one can seek his true destiny in only one way, through being who they really are. But this was no time for reflection. Destiny was beckoning him once again. He hurried quickly towards the terminal, gripping his boarding pass for Konya in one hand and feeling the slim cool outline of the bracelet in the other.

Yes, there was bound to be fear and uncertainty.

There were no guarantees, he thought, as he approached a now familiar figure standing with her back to him, making a call to someone.

He hesitated for a moment, reconsidering his decision but then strode forward. Life was always going to be a spectacle shrouded in suspense and mystery, but the adventure was well worth it! Just then his phone rang. It was Zoya.

## Bringing It to Life: Messages from Chapter Sixteen – Uncovering the Liberty of Detachment

### *The Storyline*

Richard called his father after 16 years, even though doubt crept into his mind. Earlier, Zoya had wanted to call Richard but hesitated. In both cases, they wondered what the outcome would be. But eventually, they were both able to do what they wished, despite their fears that the other person might refuse to talk.

### *Messages*

*"For success, like happiness, cannot be pursued; it must ensue, and it only does so as the unintended side-effect of one's dedication to a cause greater than oneself or as the by-product of one's surrender to a person other than oneself."*

– Viktor Frankl

### *Reflect on the following questions:*

- Do you get hurt by others' comments?

- How far are your actions governed by the fear of loss rather than the sense of doing what is right or needed?

- Can you differentiate yourself from your outcomes, goals, or vision?

- Is it your nature to do your best irrespective of the outcome?

- Do you enjoy the process or are too consumed by the fear of the outcome?

- If you have six days to live, what will be most important to you?

- When you suffer a setback do you mull over that or focus on what you learned from it?

- Do you enjoy the ride to where you are going?

- Do you realize that when you die, you don't take what you have?

Set goals, remain focused but be detached from the outcome. This creates liberty. We get attached to things, people, relationships and outcomes, assuming that these things will provide more meaning to life. However, when we get attached to outcomes, it inhibits our ability to focus on the present moment, give our full concentration to the task at hand and enjoy the process. If Richard's doubts had prevented him from calling his father, he would have missed out on reconnecting with him.

Think of past losses where you worried continually. But you managed, survived and in some cases, even thrived thereafter. Think of how a loss can possibly lead to a gain. Remember, when one door closes, another opens. But when you are too focused on the door closing, you cannot see other doors opening. Also, look at what you already have, and be grateful for it.

At the end of the day, we are all guests in this world; we will move on eventually. However, while you are here, you can leave your mark by setting goals and putting your heart, soul and body into them, and letting the outcome be the by-product of your focus.

Let your concentration be on your craft and watch the magic unfold.

### *Challenge yourself with the following 'How to' exercises:*

1) UNDERSTAND that nothing is yours, whether it is a child, a job or money. You were born with nothing and you cannot take anything with you when you die. It has been given to you as a gift during your lifetime. Enjoy it and appreciate it while you have it.

2) DIFFERENTIATE your identity from your outcomes, goals or vision. You are not your job; you are a unique, special being with good qualities regardless of your economic status, job title, marital status or religion.

3) PRACTICE doing your best. Appreciate the outcomes you achieve and understand the lessons behind the ones you did not achieve.

4) ENJOY the process – the people you come across, the lessons you learn and the precious moments in life. When you experience a mishap, look at all the good things in your life, whether they are your health, family or knowledge; there is usually something to be grateful for.

5) CHANGE the label from "defeat" to "learning and growth". If you lose someone who is close to you, you

can resign to your fate and lose out to life, or you can choose to be grateful for having the person in your life as a gift.

6) RESPOND to challenge or defeat, instead of reacting to it. Remember, you can always choose the way you respond or react.

7) FOCUS on what you need to do to achieve your goals and let go of the outcome. By doing so, you will achieve better than what you are striving to achieve.

# Conclusion

Congratulations for having read this book and absorbing some of the concepts shared here.

To keep things fresh in your mind, ponder on the 'Reflection questions' and implement the 'How to' exercises in 'Bringing it to Life: Messages from the Chapter'. If you take one chapter a week to ponder on the 'Reflections questions' and implement the 'How to' exercises, it will take you 16 weeks to complete the 16 chapters in the book. We recommend that you do this twice during the next 12 months. This will cement new habits.

If you feel you are already very good at certain concepts mentioned in the book, you can skip them. However, keep in mind that repetition is a key factor in creating new habits. New perspectives come about through changes in one's habits, not only through theory.

Learning these concepts isn't a rat-race to the finishing line and a sudden attainment of enlightenment. Rather, the journey, and how you learn these concepts, will play an important role in the development of new perspectives.

We look forward to hearing your experiences. Write to us

at info@whatyouseek.com as you implement the key lessons you have learnt in this book, including:

- being authentic and shining your light
- noticing and optimizing the positive coincidences
- achieving clarity, leading to simplicity, success and mastery
- experiencing joy and happiness in the present moment
- meditating and reducing clutter in your mind
- learning and creating meaning from tragedy
- tapping into your inner power
- converting politics into creative synergy
- realizing that receiving lightens your life
- transforming negative ego into positive pride
- understanding that fear limits your potential
- mastering the secrets of selling
- enjoying the abundance and happiness that come from giving
- living life in zest; in infinite energy and joy
- uncovering the liberty and freedom of detachment.

Embrace your journey ahead; may you discover all the hidden treasures that you are seeking. Rest assured they are seeking you too!

Sincerely,

Brian Tracy and Azim Jamal

# Acknowledgment

The fable in this book was conceived and crafted by Shailaja Sharma. She took to the project with her heart and soul. She was instrumental in thinking through the intricacies required to make the story appealing to a wide audience. We are very grateful to her for all her creative efforts. She is an excellent story writer and a great team player.

# Other Acknowledgement

We would also like to acknowledge our professional editor, Gabrielle Moss, who worked tirelessly to bring the book and fable to its current status; also Sheila Robb, Nerella Campigotto and David Rutherford, all of whom looked at various drafts and provided wise guidance, insightful input and edits to the book.

We also took feedback from team members, friends and family – too many people to name them all. We are extremely grateful for your invaluable contribution and we hope that you will take pride in being part of the success of this book.